ATHLONE RENAISSANCE LIBRARY

Selected Writings of
Fulke Greville

Selected Writings of
Fulke Greville

edited by
JOAN REES

UNIVERSITY OF LONDON
THE ATHLONE PRESS
1973

Published by
THE ATHLONE PRESS
UNIVERSITY OF LONDON
at 4 Gower Street, London WC1

Distributed by
Tiptree Book Services Ltd
Tiptree, Essex

USA & Canada
Humanities Press Inc
New York

0 485 13603 1 *cloth*
0 485 12603 6 *paperback*

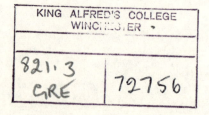
Printed in Great Britain by
WESTERN PRINTING SERVICES LTD
BRISTOL

CONTENTS

INTRODUCTION

In the old chapter house, now the vestry, of St Mary's church in Warwick there stands the very large tomb of Fulke Greville. The inscription round its sides reads: 'Fulke Greville, Servant of Queen Elizabeth, Counsellor to King James, Friend to Sir Philip Sidney'. The inscription was of Greville's own composition and it may seem brief to the point of baldness and appear to provide an inadequate summary of the life of one who lived for seventy-four years, from 1554 to 1628, was a great landowner, a distinguished courtier and statesman, and a writer whose works have never been forgotten, though the absence till recently of good modern editions and failure to appreciate their real nature has prevented their being widely read. In fact the inscription is in its way eloquent and its three terms direct us at once to the areas of Greville's life where his intellectual energies and his personal emotions were most engaged.

He went to court as a young man, full of ambition to serve his country and to make his mark in the world in some active and perhaps spectacular way. He chafed as many others did at the restrictions which Elizabeth imposed on her courtiers and when he could not get her permission to leave the country to take part in various enterprises abroad he attempted to leave without her knowledge. On one occasion he and Sidney stole away to Plymouth to join Drake with the intention of sailing with him to the West Indies. But Elizabeth firmly curbed such gestures of independence and in the end Greville resigned himself to the situation and set about making himself useful in the directions which were open to him. He represented his home county of Warwickshire in five parliaments between 1586 and 1621 (his family seat was at Alcester), and he became Treasurer of the Navy in 1598. He came to exercise considerable influence at court and it was said of him that he had the longest time without rub of any of Queen Elizabeth's favourites. His own comments on Queen Elizabeth and her policies in his writings leave no doubt that he genuinely admired and esteemed her and in the end he willingly and proudly became her 'servant'.

With the accession of James, Greville's fortunes changed. He lost his footing at court and for eleven years, from 1603–14, he was without office. During these years he acquired Warwick Castle and refurbished it, converting a neglected and decaying ruin into a splendid residence. In 1614 he was called back to office and was appointed Chancellor of the Exchequer. In 1621 he was raised to the peerage as Lord Brooke. From 1614 onwards till his death in 1628, under James and then for a few years under Charles I, he was intimately concerned with affairs of state of all kinds. But though he served James, his relation with him was never what it was with Elizabeth. In the prose work called the *Life of Sidney*, which he wrote at various times before 1614 but which prudently he did not publish in his life-time, he draws many contrasts between the statesmanship and wisdom of Elizabeth and the mismanagement and follies of James's government. 'Counsellor' to James he certainly was, having an acute sense of James's need for guidance, but he never had the confidence in him that he had had in Elizabeth and the extent of his influence on the king was strictly limited.

To have served the great queen and to have attempted, at least, to counsel James are claims to honour of which a statesman may understandably be proud and which he may well wish to commemorate on his tomb. To add to these in a brief memorial inscription, as Greville does, that he was the friend of a young man who died over forty years before at the age of thirty-two is a more surprising thing to do. Sir Philip Sidney was a remarkable phenomenon of his time. His reputation was very great, not only in this country but throughout Europe. Yet his evidently exceptional talents found little outlet during his life and when he died it was not in some glorious victory but in a minor skirmish in the wars in the Netherlands. Nevertheless, for many of his contemporaries he was the prime example of the best that Renaissance culture could produce and he was the promise of greatness to come. He appeared to be a destined leader, in politics, in religion, in the arts. When he died a great hope died with him. Greville's share in the general grief was personal and very acute. He and Sidney were the same age and had known each other since childhood. They had been to school together, gone to court together and travelled abroad together. In one of his school books

Sidney wrote one day 'Fulke Greville is a good boy' and in his early poetry he makes a number of references to their friendship and close companionship. Greville's relations with Sidney seem to have been the closest of his life and as the years passed the memory of the friend of his youth, far from weakening, took a firmer and firmer hold in Greville's mind, becoming interwoven with his most deeply held beliefs and attitudes. Sidney typified for Greville the summit of all virtue as it was attainable in this life and to have been his friend, consequently, was in his eyes one of the greatest privileges of a long and distinguished life. Greville might have said indeed that it was *the* greatest privilege and perhaps the placing of his friendship with Sidney, last of the claims to honour he makes on his tomb, is meant to give it special prominence as the apex of his career.

It was through Sidney that Greville became a poet. Thwarted by Elizabeth in his youth when he tried to see action overseas, he followed Sidney's example and turned to the writing of verse. In early days he took up, inevitably, the theme of love, but he is no writer of conventional sugared sonnets. Wit, intelligence, a sardonic and sceptical humour are hall-marks of his writing on this theme. In his love, or, as many of them are better called, anti-love poems, Greville surveys the comedy of sex relations and observes many follies, many kinds of deception and cruelty. He keeps an even pulse and an active brain. Some of these poems make striking use of religious imagery. In the earliest examples this may be no more than a familiar form of love rhetoric in which the beloved is treated as a divine or semi-divine being to be worshipped by the lover, but as time goes on the religious imagery acquires more and more serious value in Greville's poetry. The result, in the sonnet-sequence *Caelica*, is a deeply infused irony in many of the poems as if Greville were making, between the lines, something like Ben Jonson's comment on Donne's praise of Elizabeth Drury in *The Anniversary*: 'If it had been written of the Virgin Mary, it had been something.' This sharp sense of disproportion between the subject and the language applied to it contributes considerably to the disenchanted wit of many of the *Caelica* poems.

Much of Greville's writing depends on contrast as he confronts the tainted activities of the world with the absolute values of

heaven. These contrasts animate his verse treatises which gain their interest, not so much from the opposition itself, as from the range of first-hand experience on which Greville, as a practised politician, a scholar and a courtier, can draw in his presentation of worldly affairs, and from the energy of his belief in the ultimate order of God. In religion he belonged to the puritan party. He had a Calvinist sense of the sinfulness of human nature, though he did not hold a rigorous doctrine of pre-destination. On the contrary, his poetry frequently emphasises God's mercy in offering His grace to all who truly believe and repent. He had no time for the 'outward Church', i.e. all institutional religion, which he saw as deeply tainted by man's corruption. True religion, he insisted, is always 'within', an intimate matter of a man's own recognition of his sin, his heart-felt penitence, and his experience of God's mercy. In politics, Greville was a pragmatist. He preferred the monarchic to any other system of government, not because he believed in the divine right of kings but because he thought it ultimately the system by which the best balance between the interests of the governors and the governed might be achieved. His political poetry is concerned with the balancing of these interests but Greville dreams of no Utopias and is fundamentally sceptical about what can be achieved in human life and with human material. His writing is full of matter and the treatises, which deal with moral, political, and religious themes, present an acute and comprehensive analysis of the subjects he treats, illuminated from time to time by prophetic fire as he denounces the corruptions of man or speaks with feeling of the mercies of God.

Greville's poetry traces the flaw of sin which runs through all human experience, whether in state affairs, in personal relationships, or in intellectual activities. Recognition of this flaw and of man's need for redemption constitutes the essence of wisdom as Greville grew to understand it and poetry became for him an instrument by which this truth could be mediated to men. Though he claims no compelling personal impulse urging him to write (having, as he tells us, embarked on poetry in imitation of Sidney's example), yet he had from the beginning considerable literary gifts: his mind was fertile in images and the earlier *Caelica* poems show him to be witty and skilful in adapting to his own tone and purposes the lyrical models of his time. As he grew

older his style became more severe but his mature concern was always with 'truth' as he conceived it, not with lyric facility, or beauty for its own sake. Sidney wished to win a higher esteem and dignity for poetry: Greville also worked to enhance the status of verse, making it a medium for his serious purposes, but he pursued his objective with a rigour which distinguishes him from his more graceful and lighter-handed friend; but Sidney, after all, died when both he and Greville were young.

'Nature never set forth the earth in so rich tapestry as divers poets have done', wrote Sidney, celebrating the joyous creative power of poetry, 'neither with pleasant rivers, fruitful trees, sweet-smelling flowers, nor whatsoever else may make the too-much-loved earth more lovely.' Greville's art is also creative, but it is not a golden world which he offers us. His world combines rather an acute and cool-headed analysis of what men do (as distinct from what they ought to do) and a fervent awareness of another dimension of experience in which selfish hope and fear give way to absolute confidence in a Divine providence. One or the other of these elements may at times predominate in his poetry but often his eminently strong and serious intelligence binds them both together in an unusual and impressive compound.

His greatest achievement is his evolution of a language of multiple reference by which he can present experience in its secular and its divine contexts simultaneously. Greville is continuously conscious of the dual nature of experience. He sees and studies and to some degree participates in the desire for power in politics and gratification in love, but even while he makes his shrewd and far-ranging commentary and offers the fruits of his experience in these matters, he remembers another scale of values by which all the activities of the world are without merit and most of them are misdirected. In some of his most characteristic poems, the language he uses both describes human activity as it is and at the same time supplies a context in which it is judged in terms of divine order and divine law. This is true of some of the *Caelica* poems, and the play *Mustapha* is an example on an extended scale. This play is printed here in full because, folded layer upon layer within its story of the contemporary east, is the full extent of Greville's commentary on his experience of life. *Mustapha* is about

political behaviour; it also studies the passions by which individual conduct is motivated; and, its third and underlying level
of meaning, it places its protagonists in situations where they
must choose their deepest commitment—to God, or to the world,
the flesh and the devil. Using the form of non-theatrical drama
deriving from the Latin dramatist Seneca, Greville achieves in
this play a remarkable fashioning of complex and profound
matter. The two choruses which come together at the end of the
last act compose between them one of the most striking and
effective of all Greville's commentaries on the human condition.
On the one hand are those (in the play they are Tartars) who
have no religious feeling whatever and who bid their fellow-men
follow what they call 'nature', urging them to make much of life
in this world and to seek tangible goods. On the other are those,
like the priests of the play, who, having some religious awareness,
wish for faith but cannot quite achieve it. In their heart of hearts
they know that they are not themselves convinced of the truth of
what they preach. For them, beset by the conflicting claims of the
world and the spirit, the condition of humanity is indeed 'wearisome' and there is no escape from the impotence and frustrations
of their position.

The influence of Seneca in the sixteenth century developed in
two principal directions. On the one hand his use of sensational
plots—*Hercules Furens*, for example, or *Medea*—encouraged
dramatists to fill their plays with exciting theatrical effects.
Shakespeare's *Titus Andronicus* and Kyd's *The Spanish Tragedy*
show the influence of this theatrical Senecanism. To others, however, Seneca appeared as a much more academic dramatist, a
writer who observed the unities of time, place and action and
substituted 'stately speeches and well-sounding phrases' for crude
physical activity. Sidney saw him in this way (the phrase quoted
comes from his *Apology for Poetry*), and after Sidney's death his
sister, the Countess of Pembroke, tried to counter the rise of
theatrical drama by writing and encouraging others to write
'closet' (i.e. non-theatrical) drama in the Senecan rhetorical
mode. Greville was one of these. He did not intend his plays for
the stage but he recognised the possibilities offered by non-
theatrical drama for the exploration and amplification of
situations and he exploited them with a profundity and intellec-

tual vigour which make *Alaham* and *Mustapha*, his two surviving dramas, remarkable productions.

Greville is often a difficult poet, especially in his non-lyrical work and especially at first encounter. His material ranges widely, is deeply pondered and demands intellectual engagement on the part of the reader. His endeavour is to express concisely and strongly what he thinks energetically and feels urgently and a very distinctive kind of language is created by these pressures upon his verse. This language includes a considerable proportion of abstract words, endowed by his use of them with a high charge of meaning. These sometimes help him to a lapidary formulation which is pointed and economical, as in the cynical 'Repentance still becomes desire's mother' (*Caelica* XI), or the ominous 'Change hath prepared her moulds for innovation' (*Mustapha* I. ii. 208).[1] Sometimes, however, the level of abstraction is several stages removed from an immediately accessible meaning and the reader has to make a continual effort to find solid ground beneath his feet. A similar kind of exertion is called for in response to Greville's use of metaphor. He makes abundant use of imagery but the effect is not primarily or directly to stir the imagination but rather to stimulate the mind. Continuous mental activity is required to identify the point of correspondence from which the metaphor derives and to recognise the implications of the allusion. Lines 57–108 of the first chorus of *Mustapha* may stand as an example of a typical piece of Greville's discursive writing. The passage constitutes a corrosive analysis of the 'arts of tyranny' and of men's connivance at their own enslavement. The imagery is packed close but the images are not coherent: one does not enrich or expand another but is simply different, invoking a new sector of experience and discarding the last. For example, the wood and the axe of ll. 75–6 give way to imagery of beasts in ll. 79–82 and the underlying literal meaning of the lines taken together must be understood to relate to 'lifting tyrants higher.[2] These image

---

[1] Greville's writing abounds in aphorisms and the pages of the early editions are peppered with italicised *sententiae*. His friend, Sir Francis Bacon, who was a keen collector of aphorisms, includes two spoken examples by Greville in his *Apophthegms* (nos. 202 and 235 in *Philosophical Works of Bacon*, ed. J. M. Robertson, London, 1905, pp. 881 and 883).

[2] In fact in the Warwick ms. ll. 75–8, which contain the axe image, have

sequences may be quite long and the effort of taking the point of the successive terms and of following the train of thought which winds through them may be strenuous for the reader.

A shorter example of the same kind of thing occurs in the stanza beginning at l. 85 of the Second Chorus of *Mustapha*. The subject is a comparison, from the point of view of Mahometan priests, of the Christian and the Turkish polity. The priests speak disparagingly of the Christians' interest in theoretic knowledge and also of their delicacy of body, and they go on:

> Yet by our traffic with this dreaming nation,
> Their conquered vice hath stained our conquering state,
> And brought thin cobwebs into reputation,
> Of tender subtlety; whose stepmother, Fate,
> So inlays courage with ill-shadowing fear,
> As makes it much more hard to do than bear.

'Dreaming nation' stresses the opinion the Turks hold that their enemies are lacking in vigour and the will to action. The play on 'conquered 'and 'conquering' points the paradox that the victors in battle are corrupted by the weaknesses of their opponents. The phrase 'thin cobwebs . . . of tender subtlety' describes the fine-drawn intellectualism of the West. 'Whose' in l.88 refers to 'our conquering state'. Fate is a 'stepmother' because its actions (like those of Rossa in the play) are malicious. Fear is 'ill-shadowing' because it bodes ill for the success of any action, and when it is 'inlaid' with courage it will counteract the bolder impulse till the point at which it becomes easier to suffer passively than to take decisive action.

This stanza is very compressed indeed. Images and ideas cluster thickly together and the reader must engage, like the poet, in vigorous moment by moment mental activity while at the same time he endeavours to keep the connections of the argument constantly clear in his head, Here as elsewhere, the difficulties of the progress are suddenly illuminated by a splendid line or two:

> 'He whom God chooseth out of doubt doth well:
> What they that choose their God do, who can tell?'

lines drawn through them as if Greville himself at some stage decided to curtail the run of images. The passage as printed in the 1633 folio is nevertheless a fair example of a characteristic kind of writing.

There are times, certainly, when the poet seems to be trying to carve his verses out against the grain of language and there is little profit or pleasure in the process; but there are many other passages which reveal themselves as a rich web of idea and illustration. Greville's discursive writing embodies a mode of concentrated thinking and once the thought process which his lines articulate becomes familiar the very remarkable style with its ironies, abstractions, images, compressed or strained syntax, often justifies itself as the medium of a highly individual and strongly marked mind and personality.

Greville is not always difficult. He has a considerable repertory of poetic effects. Sonnet L of *Caelica* is direct enough and there are moments in *Alaham* where the horrors of the action are heightened by a ruthless baldness of statement. He can also produce gentler effects— though we are rarely allowed to take them in the end quite at face value: for example, *Caelica* XXII. When he writes in the last poems of the *Caelica* sequence of his experience of sin and the saving might of Christ he writes with subtlety still but also with power and personal intensity, making use of the architectonics of the verse forms and the resonance of language to produce poems which are deeply impressive.

Greville was a man committed to the world by those aspects of his temperament which made him a successful courtier and minister of state and enabled him to rise to power and keep it under James, in spite of powerful forces which worked against him at the beginning of the reign and in spite also of his own critical awareness of the king's shortcomings. He was also a man in whom a sense of the vanity of the world and the need for God's grace to redeem our fallen nature grew ever stronger, nourished especially, it would seem, by the defeat of early hopes and ambitions when Sidney died. He knew the world and believed in God: these two characteristics were not at war in him but re-inforced each other. In proportion as he understood very clearly what constitutes efficiency and success in wordly affairs, so the unworldly qualities of unselfishness, renunciation and obedience to a higher law shone the more brightly for him. Such a personality may appear enigmatic. To run so energetically in life in a race whose prizes he always described in his writing as unworthy and gained only by muddy ways may seem morally ambiguous and perhaps to indicate plain dishonesty. In Greville it was not so. He believed that the corruptions of the world were inevitable because of man's fall from his primal innocence but he believed that no man has the right to withdraw from it, except perhaps the rare few who are especially endowed with spiritual purity, and they will not so much withdraw as be rejected by the world. He did not count himself among these. His part was to master the ways of the world as best he could, while at the same time never losing sight of its vanity and always aspiring to greater spiritual grace.

Greville died by violence. In his seventy-fifth year he was stabbed one day by a servant who was discontented, so the unsubstantiated story of the time went, because Greville had not made provision that he thought suitable for him in his will. This occurred in London. The servant immediately afterwards stabbed himself and died. Greville lingered on for a month, but in October 1628 his body was brought to Warwick and ceremonially buried in St Mary's church. For his tomb he selected the titles of honour which epitomised his life as the world at large might know it. His writings he left for posterity for he published none of them in his lifetime. Through them it may be that we have a deeper insight into the strong mind and striking personality of this remarkable man than anyone of his own time did.

In the selections which follow, all the kinds of Greville's writing are represented: short lyrics (the *Caelica* sequence), verse treatises (on monarchy, human learning, fame and honour, wars and religion), Senecan plays (*Alaham* and *Mustapha*) and prose (the *Life of Sidney*). A brief introduction is given before each text and fuller commentaries, together with notes on particular points in the text, are given at the end of the volume.

CHRONOLOGICAL TABLE

1554 Fulke Greville born at Beauchamp's Court, Alcester, Warwickshire.

Philip Sidney born.

1564 Greville enters Shrewsbury School.

Sidney enters on the same day.

Shakespeare born, Stratford-upon-Avon.

1568 Greville enters Jesus College, Cambridge.

1575 He probably makes his first appearance at Court, together with Sidney.

1577 Greville sent by the Queen, with Sidney, on a mission to Germany and the Netherlands.

1578 Greville volunteers for service in the Netherlands wars but is stopped by the Queen on the point of embarkation.

1580 He is given command of a ship guarding the Irish coast against an expected Spanish landing.

Sidney writes his *Apology for Poetry*.

1581 Greville sits in Parliament as member for Southampton but the election is later declared invalid.

1583 Giordano Bruno, an Italian philosopher, famous for his forward-looking, unconventional thought, visits England.

Sidney marries Frances Walsingham.

1584 Greville elected as M.P. for Heydon in Yorkshire.

Greville and Sidney entertain Bruno to supper on Ash Wednesday. An account of the evening is given in Bruno's *La Cena de le Ceneri*.

1585 Greville and Sidney attempt to join Drake on an expedition to the West Indies but are prevented by the Queen.

Sidney appointed Governor of Flushing in the Netherlands.

1586 Greville elected to represent Warwickshire in Parliament. (He continues to sit for Warwickshire in successive Parliaments till 1601 and again in 1621.)

Sidney dies of wounds in the Netherlands in October.

1587 Greville serves under Henry of Navarre (later Henry IV) in France.

1588 The Spanish Armada.

1590 Greville holds the offices of Clerk of the Council in the Marches of Wales, Clerk of the Signet and Secretary. He edits Sidney's *Arcadia* from a revised text left in his care by Sidney on his departure for the Netherlands.

1591 First (pirated) edition of Sidney's *Astrophil and Stella* published, together with some of Samuel Daniel's *Delia* sonnets.

1596 Robert Cecil becomes Secretary of State. After James's accession Cecil seems to have been largely responsible for keeping Greville out of office.

1597 Essex's expedition to Cadiz. Greville, a close friend, is employed to take the Queen's licence for departure to Essex at Plymouth.

1597 Essex undertakes the unsuccessful Islands Voyage.

1598 Greville appointed Treasurer of the Navy.

1599 He is appointed rear-admiral in command of the largest vessel of the fleet: a Spanish attack expected.

Essex appointed Lord Deputy in Ireland but returns to England against instructions in September.

Samuel Daniel publishes *Musophilus*, a poem in defence of learning, in which he acknowledges Greville's encouragement to write a 'poem of discourse'.

1601 Essex's rising, his trial and execution.

1603 Death of Queen Elizabeth and accession of James I.

Greville made a Knight of the Bath at James's coronation.

1604 Greville obliged to surrender his Treasurership of the Navy. He is granted Warwick Castle.

1605 Samuel Daniel, who has been closely associated with Greville, is called before the Privy Council on suspicion of having made hostile comment on the government's conduct of the Essex case in his neo-classical play, *Philotas*.

Bacon's *Advancement of Learning* published, a work which may have been in Greville's mind when he wrote his treatise *Of Human Learning*.

1606 Greville's father dies.

1609 A pirated edition of *Mustapha* published.

1612 Robert Cecil (Earl of Salisbury) dies.

1614 Greville becomes Chancellor and Under-Treasurer of the Exchequer.

1616   George Villiers, a favourite of James I, created Baron and Viscount Buckingham.

Shakespeare dies.

1617   Greville entertains James I at Warwick.

1621   He is raised to the peerage as Baron Brooke. He ceases to be Chancellor of the Exchequer.

1625   Death of James I and accession of Charles I.

1628   Duke of Buckingham assassinated in August.

Greville fatally stabbed by a servant and dies in London on 30 September. Buried in St Mary's Church, Warwick.

BIBLIOGRAPHY

The editions of Greville's works by Geoffrey Bullough and G. A. Wilkes provide much useful information. For the political background of Greville's thought, J. W. Allen's *A History of Political Thought in the Sixteenth Century* (London, 1928) is a standard general study and there are two articles by H. N. Maclean published in *Huntington Library Quarterly*: 'Fulke Greville: Kingship and Sovereignty' (xvi (1953), 237–71) and 'Fulke Greville on War' (xxi (1957–8), 95–109). For the history of the Puritan movement in the sixteenth century Patrick Collinson's *The Elizabethan Puritan Movement* (London, 1967) may be consulted. There is a valuable study of Calvin by F. Wendel (*Calvin*, Fontana Library, 1965) and the edition of Spenser's *Fowre Hymnes* and *Epithalamion* by Enid Welsford (Oxford, 1967) contains a useful account of neo-Platonism and the Protestant background of Spenser's thought which is relevant also to Greville. A critical biography of Greville by Joan Rees, *Fulke Greville, Lord Brooke* (London, 1971), gives special attention to Greville's themes and his qualities as a writer. The historical background of Greville's work is treated in detail in *The Life of Fulke Greville* by R. A. Rebholz (Oxford, 1971). Una Ellis Fermor's book *The Jacobean Drama* (London, 1936) includes a chapter on Greville's plays.

TEXTUAL NOTE

With the exception of a few of the *Caelica* poems and a pirated edition of *Mustapha* in 1609, none of Greville's work was published in his life-time. The best modern editions are those of Geoffrey Bullough, *Poems and Dramas of Fulke Greville*, 2 vols. (Edinburgh and London, 1939); G. A. Wilkes, *The Remains* (Oxford, 1965); and Nowell Smith, *Life of Sir Philip Sidney* (Oxford, 1907). In the preparation of the present selection, I have made an independent collation of the early editions and manuscripts but I have accepted the decisions of the editors named above about copy-text. On a few occasions I prefer a different reading and these are listed at the end of this section. Spelling and punctuation have been modernised.

There is very little evidence for the order of composition of Greville's work but he engaged in fairly extensive revisions over what may have been a considerable number of years. It would be impracticable to provide a full textual apparatus in a volume of this nature but the commentary includes notes of variant readings where these are of special interest. These occur mainly in relation to *Mustapha* which exists in two substantially different versions.

The early editions and the manuscripts are as follows:

Editions

(i) *Certain Learned and Elegant Works*, 1633: comprising the treatises of *Human Learning, Fame and Honour*, and *Wars*; the plays *Alaham* and *Mustapha*; the sonnet sequence *Caelica*; the letters *To an Honourable Lady* and *Of Travel* (neither of these letters is represented in these selections).

(ii) *The Remains*, 1670: comprising the treatises of *Monarchy* and *Religion*.

(iii) *Life of Sir Philip Sidney*, 1652.

(iv) *Mustapha*, 1609, ed. N. Butter (an unauthorised edition).

Manuscripts

(i) The Warwick manuscripts. These mss., formerly at Warwick Castle, now in the British Museum, contain scribal copies of all

Greville's poetical works and the letter *To an Honourable Lady*.

(ii) A manuscript copy of parts of the treatise of *Monarchy* in the possession of Harvard College Library.

(iii) *Mustapha*. Manuscripts in: (a) Trinity College, Cambridge; (b) The Folger Shakespeare Library, Washington.

(iv) *Life of Sidney*. Manuscripts in: (a) Trinity College, Cambridge; (b) Shrewsbury Public Library. The ms. at Shrewsbury has come to light since Nowell Smith's edition was prepared and hence was not collated by him. It has been described by S. Blaine Ewing, 'A new manuscript of Greville's *Life of Sidney*', *Modern Language Review* xlix (1954), 424–7.

W   Warwick mss.
F   edition of 1633
C   Cambridge ms. of *Mustapha*
Folger   Folger Library ms. of *Mustapha*
Q   1609 edition of *Mustapha*
Bullough   *Poems and Dramas of Fulke Greville*

Readings of this edition

Caelica
33 (XCI) 12 raiseth] W; riseth F and Bullough.
34 (XCIV) 16 each] W; earthy F; earth Bullough.

Mustapha
I. i. 93 youths] W and F; youth Bullough.
  ii. 135 form] W and F; forms Bullough.
260 knows] W and F; know Bullough.
II. i. 54 ever, lives] C, Folger, W; lives, ever, F, Q and Bullough.
  ii. 49 estate] W; estates F and Bullough.

Chorus Tertius l.119 though] W and F; thought Bullough.
Chorus Quartus l.14 Yea] W and F; yet Bullough.
  l.26 power of thrones] W; power of the thrones F and Bullough.
  l.105 is] W; as F and Bullough.
V. iii. 63 his] W and F; this Bullough.
Chorus Sacerdotum l.15 we] C, Folger; is Q, F and Bullough.
  l.21 God and stir] C and Folger; good and still Q, F, and Bullough.

CAELICA

The sequence consists of 109 short poems, of which 41 are sonnets. The sonnets are constructed as three quatrains and a couplet, but there is often a break in movement before the sestet, as in the Italian sonnet, and in a few poems Greville reduces the number of rhymes from the seven of the Shakespearean form to five, or even three. Most of the other poems are composed in stanzas of four or six lines. There is evidence that the first 76 poems were written before Sidney's death in 1586 but Greville may have gone on revising and composing until the end of his life. Three women's names are mentioned in the sequence, Caelica, Myra and Cynthia, but whether they denote three different women, or one under different names, or whether any real woman was intended at all, we do not know. The love poems illustrate a variety of moods, from idealism to cynicism, but an active and subtle intelligence rather than warm sentiment characterises them. Some poems make penetrating comment on political themes and in the later part of the sequence religious motifs predominate. These draw out and carry to their conclusion ideas implicit in the love poems where theological references often occur, as if Greville were matching the extravagances of devotion to a mistress against the claims to worship of God.

1 · (I)*

Love, the delight of all well-thinking minds,
Delight, the fruit of virtue dearly loved,
Virtue, the highest good that reason finds,
Reason, the fire wherein men's thoughts be proved,
Are from the world by Nature's power bereft,
And in one creature, for her glory, left.

Beauty her cover is, the eye's true pleasure;
In honour's fame she lives, the ear's sweet music;
Excess of wonder grows from her true measure;
Her worth is passion's wound and passion's physic;   10
From her true heart clear springs of wisdom flow,
Which imaged in her words and deeds men know.

* The figure in brackets denotes the number of the poem in the complete sequence.

Time fain would stay, that she might never leave her,
Place doth rejoice that she must needs contain her,
Death craves of heaven that she may not bereave her,
The heavens know their own and do maintain her;
Delight, love, reason, virtue let it be
To set all women light but only she.

2 · (III)

More than most fair, full of that heavenly fire
Kindled above to show the Maker's glory,
Beauty's first-born, in whom all powers conspire
To write the Graces' life, and Muses' story.
If in my heart all saints else be defaced,
Honour the shrine, where you alone are placed.

Thou window of the sky and pride of spirits,
True character of honour in perfection,
Thou heavenly creature, judge of earthly merits,
And glorious prison of man's pure affection,   10
If in my heart all nymphs else be defaced,
Honour the shrine, where you alone are placed.

3 · (IV)

You little stars that live in skies,
And glory in Apollo's glory,
In whose aspects conjoynèd lies
The heavens' will, and nature's story,
Joy to be likened to those eyes,
Which eyes make all eyes glad, or sorry,
For when you force thoughts from above,
These over-rule your force by love.

And thou O Love, which in these eyes
Hast married Reason with Affection,   10
And made them saints of beauty's skies,
Where joys are shadows of perfection,

Lend me thy wings that I may rise
Up not by worth but thy election;
For I have vowed in strangest fashion,
To love, and never seek compassion.

4 · (X)

Love, of man's wandering thoughts the restless being,
Thou from my mind with glory wast invited,
Glory of those fair eyes, where all eyes, seeing
Virtue's and beauty's riches, are delighted;
What angels' pride, or what self-disagreeing,
What dazzling brightness hath your beams benighted,
That fall'n thus from those joys which you aspired,
Down to my darkened mind you are retired?

Within which mind since you from thence ascended,
Truth clouds itself, Wit serves but to resemble,   10
Envy is king, at others' good offended,
Memory doth worlds of wretchedness assemble,
Passion to ruin passion is intended,
My reason is but power to dissemble;
Then tell me Love, what glory you divine
Yourself can find within this soul of mine?

Rather go back unto that heavenly quire
Of Nature's riches, in her beauties placed,
And there in contemplation feed desire,
Which till it wonder, is not rightly graced;   20
For those sweet glories, which you do aspire,
Must as Ideas only be embraced,
Since excellence in other form enjoyed,
Is, by descending to her saints, destroyed.

5 · (XI)

Juno, that on her head Love's livery carried,
Scorning to wear the marks of Io's pleasure,
Knew while the boy in equinoctial tarried,

His heats would rob the heaven of heavenly treasure;
Beyond the tropics she the boy doth banish,
Where smokes must warm before his fire do blaze,
And children's thoughts not instantly grow mannish,
Fear keeping lust there very long at gaze:
But see how that poor goddess was deceived,
For women's hearts far colder there than ice,   10
When once the fire of lust they have received,
With two extremes so multiply the vice,
As neither party satisfying other,
Repentance still becomes desire's mother.

6 · (XVIII)

I offer wrong to my beloved saint,
I scorn, I change, I falsify my love,
Absence and time have made my homage faint,
With Cupid I do everywhere remove.
I sigh, I sorrow, I do play the fool,
Mine eyes like weather-cocks on her attend:
Zeal thus on either side she puts to school,
That will needs have inconstancy to friend.
I grudge, she saith, that many should adore her,
Where love doth suffer, and think all things meet;   10
She saith, All self-ness must fall down before her:
I say, Where is the sauce should make that sweet?
Change and contempt (you know) ill speakers be,
Caelica: and such are all your thoughts of me.

7 · (XXI)

Satan, no woman, yet a wand'ring spirit,
When he saw ships sail two ways with one wind,
Of sailors' trade he hell did disinherit:
The devil himself loves not a half-fast mind.
The satyr when he saw the shepherd blow
To warm his hands, and make his pottage cool,
Manhood foreswears, and half a beast did know,
Nature with double breath is put to school.

Cupid doth head his shafts in women's faces,
Where smiles and tears dwell ever near together,   10
Where all the arts of change give passion graces;
While these clouds threaten, who fears not the weather?
Sailors and satyrs, Cupid's knights and I,
Fear women that swear, Nay; and know they lie.

8 · (XXII)

I with whose colours Myra dressed her head,
I, that ware posies of her own hand making,
I, that mine own name in the chimneys read
By Myra finely wrought ere I was waking:
Must I look on, in hope time coming may
With change bring back my turn again to play?

I, that on Sunday at the church-stile found
A garland sweet, with true-love knots in flowers,
Which I to wear about mine arm was bound
That each of us might know that all was ours: 10
Must I now lead an idle life in wishes?
And follow Cupid for his loaves and fishes?

I, that did wear the ring her mother left,
I, for whose love she gloried to be blamed,
I, with whose eyes her eyes committed theft,
I, who did make her blush when I was named;
Must I lose ring, flowers, blush, theft and go naked,
Watching with sighs, till dead love be awakèd?

I, that when drowsy Argus fell asleep,
Like Jealousy o'erwatchèd with desire,   20
Was even warnèd modesty to keep,
While her breath, speaking, kindled nature's fire:
Must I look on a-cold, while others warm them?
Do Vulcan's brothers in such fine nets arm them?

Was it for this that I might Myra see
Washing the water with her beauties, white?

Yet would she never write her love to me;
Thinks wit of change while thoughts are in delight?
Mad girls must safely love, as they may leave,
No man can print a kiss, lines may deceive.   30

9 · (XXXVI)

Kings that in youth, like all things else, are fine,
Have some who for their childish faults are beaten;
When more years unto greater vice incline
Some whom the world doth, for their errors, threaten:
So Cupid, you, who boast of princes' blood,
For women's prince-like weaknesses are blamed,
And common error, yet not understood,
Makes you, for their new-fangledness, defamed.
Poor women swear they, ignorant of harms,
With gentle minds perchance take easy motions;   10
Sweet nature yielding to the pleasing charms
Of man's false lust disguisèd with devotion;
But which are worse, kings ill, or easily led,
Schools of this truth are yet not brought a-bed.

10 · (XXXIX)

The pride of flesh, by reach of human wit,
Did purpose once to over-reach the sky;
And where before God drowned the world for it,
Yet Babylon it built up, not to die.
God knew these fools how foolishly they wrought,
That destiny with policy would break,
Straight none could tell his fellow what he thought,
Their tongues were changed, and men not taught to speak:
So I, that heavenly peace would comprehend,
In mortal seat of Caelica's fair heart,   10
To babylon my self there did intend,
With natural kindness, and with passion's art:
But when I thought myself of her self free,
All's changed: she understands all men but me.

11 · (XL)

The nurse-life wheat, within his green husk growing,
Flatters our hope and tickles our desire,
Nature's true riches in sweet beauties showing,
Which sets all hearts, with labour's love, on fire.
No less fair is the wheat when golden ear
Shows unto hope the joys of near enjoying:
Fair and sweet is the bud, more sweet and fair
The rose, which proves that time is not destroying.
Caelica, your youth, the morning of delight,
Enamell'd o'er with beauties white and red,   10
All sense and thoughts did to belief invite
That Love and Glory there are brought to bed;
And your ripe years' love-noon (he goes no higher)
Turns all the spirits of man into desire.

12 · (XLIV)

The golden-age was when the world was young,
Nature so rich, as earth did need no sowing,
Malice not known, the serpents had not stung,
Wit was but sweet affection's overflowing.

Desire was free, and Beauty's first begotten;
Beauty then neither net, nor made by art,
Words out of thoughts brought forth, and not forgotten,
The Laws were inward that did rule the heart.

The brazen age is now when earth is worn,
Beauty grown sick, Nature corrupt and nought,   10
Pleasure untimely dead as soon as born,
Both words and kindness strangers to our thought:

If now this changing world do change her head,
Caelica, what have her new lords for to boast?
The old lord knows desire is poorly fed,
And sorrows not a wavering province lost,

Since in the gilt-age Saturn ruled alone,
And in this painted, planets every one.

13 · (L)

Scoggin his wife by chance mistook her bed;
Such chances oft befall poor women-kind,
Alas poor souls, for when they miss their head,
What marvel is it, though the rest be blind?

This bed it was a lord's bed where she light,
Who nobly pitying this poor woman's hap,
Gave alms both to relieve and to delight,
And made the golden shower fall on her lap.

Then in a freedom asks her as they lay,
Whose were her lips and breasts: and she sware, His: 10
For hearts are open when thoughts fall to play.
At last he asks her, Whose her backside is?
She vowed that it was Scoggin's only part,
Who never yet came nearer to her heart.

Scoggin o'erheard; but taught by common use,
That he who sees all those which do him harm,
Or will in marriage boast such small abuse,
Shall never have his night-gown furrèd warm:
And was content, since all was done in play,
To know his luck, and bear his arms away.   20

Yet when his wife should to the market go,
Her breast and belly he in canvas drest,
And on her backside fine silk did bestow,
Joying to see it braver than the rest.

His neighbours asked him, Why? and Scoggin sware,
That part of all his wife was only his:
The lord should deck the rest, to whom they are,
For he knew not what lordly-fashion is.
If husbands now should only deck their own,
Silk would make many by their backs be known.   30

...er hinders love and hate.
...can well behold with eyes,
...what underneath him lies.

16 · (LVIII)

...tree in youth proud of his leaves and springs,
...body shadowed in his glory lays;
...none do fly with art, or others' wings,
...they in whom all, save desire, decays;
...in in age, when no leaves on them grow,
...n borrow they their green of mistletoe.

...ere Caelica, when she was young and sweet,
...rned her head with golden borrowed hair
...hide her own for cold, she thinks it meet
...e head should mourn that all the rest was fair: 10
...d now in age when outward things decay,
...spite of age, she throws that hair away.

...hose golden hairs she then used but to tie
...or captived souls which she in triumph led,
...ho not content the sun's fair light to eye,
...ithin his glory their sense dazzlèd:
...nd now again her own black hair puts on,
...o mourn for thoughts by her worths overthrown.

17 · (LIX)

...ho ever sails near to Bermuda coast,
...oes hard aboard the monarchy of fear,
...here all desires (but life's desire) are lost,
...or wealth and fame put off their glories there.

...et this isle poison-like, by mischief known,
...eans not desire from her sweet nurse, the sea;
...ut unseen shows us where our hopes be sown,
...ith woeful signs declaring joyful way.
...or who will seek the wealth of western sun,
...ft by Bermuda's miseries must run.   10

14 · (LII)

Away with these self-loving lads,
Whom Cupid's arrow never glads:
Away poor souls, that sigh and weep,
In love of those that lie asleep:
For Cupid is a meadow-god,
And forceth none to kiss the rod.

Sweet Cupid's shafts like destiny
Do causeless good or ill decree;
Desert is born out of his bow,
Reward upon his wing doth go;   10
What fools are they that have not known,
That Love likes no laws but his own.

My songs they be of Cynthia's praise,
I wear her rings on holy days,
In every tree I write her name,
And every day I read the same.
Where honour Cupid's rival is
There miracles are seen of his.

If Cynthia crave her ring of me,
I blot her name out of the tree,   20
If doubt do darken things held dear,
Then well-fare Nothing once a year;
For many run, but one must win,
Fools only hedge the cuckoo in.

The worth that worthiness should move,
Is Love, that is the bow of love,
And Love as well thee foster can,
As can the mighty nobleman.
Sweet saint 'tis true, you worthy be,
Yet without love nought worth to me.   30

15 · (LVI)

All my senses, like beacon's flame,
Gave alarum to desire
To take arms in Cynthia's name,
And set all my thoughts on fire:
Fury's wit persuaded me,
Happy love was hazard's heir,
Cupid did best shoot and see
In the night where smooth is fair;
Up I start believing well
To see if Cynthia were awake;   10
Wonders I saw, who can tell?
And thus unto myself I spake:
'Sweet God Cupid where am I,
That by pale Diana's light
Such rich beauties do espy,
As harm our senses with delight?
Am I borne up to the skies?
See where Jove and Venus shine,
Showing in her heavenly eyes
That desire is divine: 20
Look where lies the milken way,
Way unto that dainty throne,
Where while all the gods would play,
Vulcan thinks to dwell alone.
Shadowing it with curious art,
Nets of sullen golden hair.
Mars am I and may not part
Till that I be taken there.'
Therewithal I heard a sound,
Made of all the parts of love,   30
Which did sense delight and wound.
Planets with such music move.
Those joys drew desires near,
The heavens blushed, the white showed red,
Such red as in skies appear
When Sol parts from Thetis' bed.

Then unto myself I said,
'Surely I Apollo am,
Yonder is the glorious maid
Which men do Aurora name,
Who for pride she hath in me
Blushing forth desire and fear,
While she would have no man see,
Makes the world know I am there.'
I resolve to play my son
And misguide my chariot fire,
All the sky to overcome
And enflame with my desire.
I gave reins to this conceit,
Hope went on the wheels of lust:
Fancy's scales are false of weight,
Thoughts take thought that go of trust.
I stepped forth to touch the sky,
I a god by Cupid dreams,
Cynthia who did naked lie
Runs away like silver streams,
Leaving hollow banks behind,
Who can neither forward move,
Nor, if rivers be unkind,
Turn away or leave to love.
There stand I, like Arctic pole,
Where Sol passeth o'er the line,
Mourning my benighted soul,
Which so loseth light divine.
There stand I like men that preach
From the execution place,
At their death content to teach
All the world with their disgrace:
He that lets his Cynthia lie,
Naked on a bed of play,
To say prayers ere she die,
Teacheth time to run away.
Let no love-desiring heart,
In the stars go seek his fate,
Love is only Nature's art,

Who seeks the God of Love, in Beauty's sky,
Must pass the Empire of confusèd Passion,
Where our desires to all but horrors die,
Before that joy and peace can take their fashion.

Yet this fair heaven that yields this soul-despair,
Weans not the heart from his sweet god, Affection;
But rather shows us what sweet joys are there,
Where constancy is servant to perfection.
Who Caelica's chaste heart then seeks to move,
Must joy to suffer all the woes of love.   20

18 · (LX)

Caelica, you said I do obscurely live,
Strange to my friends, with strangers in suspect,
(For darkness doth suspicion ever give,
Of hate to men or too much self-respect):
Fame, you do say, with many wings doth fly,
Who leaves himself, you say, doth living die.

Caelica, 'tis true, I do in darkness go.
Honour I seek not, nor hunt after fame:
I am thought-bound, I do not long to know,
I feel within, what men without me blame: 10
I scorn the world, the world scorns me, 'tis true;
What can a heart do more to honour you?

Knowledge and fame in open hearts do live,
Honour is pure hearts' homage unto these,
Affection all men unto beauty give,
And by that law enjoynèd are to please:
The world in two I have divided fit;
Myself to you, and all the rest to it.

19 · (LXI)

Caelica, while you do swear you love me best,
And ever lovèd only me,
I feel that all powers are opprest
By love, and love by destiny.

For as the child in swaddling bands,
When it doth see the nurse come nigh,
With smiles and crows doth lift the hands,
Yet still must in the cradle lie:
So in the boat of fate I row,
And looking to you, from you go.   10

When I see in thy once-belovèd brows,
The heavy marks of constant love,
I call to mind my broken vows,
And child-like to the nurse would move;

But love is of the phoenix-kind,
And burns itself in self-made fire,
To breed still new birds in the mind,
From ashes of the old desire:
And hath his wings from constancy,
As mountains called of moving be.   20

Then Caelica lose not heart-eloquence,
Love understands not 'come again':
Who changes in her own defence,
Needs not cry to the deaf in vain.

Love is no true made looking-glass,
Which perfect yields the shape we bring,
It ugly shows us all that was,
And flatters every future thing.
When Phoebus' beams no more appear,
'Tis darker that the day was here.   30

Change, I confess, it is a hateful power,
To them that all at once must think,
Yet nature made both sweet and sour,
She gave the eye a lid to wink:

And though the youth that are estranged
From mother's lap to other skies,
Do think that nature there is changed
Because at home their knowledge lies;
Yet shall they see who far have gone,
That pleasure speaks more tongues than one.   40

The leaves fall off when sap goes to the root,
The warmth doth clothe the bough again;
But to the dead tree what doth boot
The silly man's manuring pain?

Unkindness may piece up again,
But kindness either changed or dead,
Self-pity may in fools complain;
Put thou thy horns on other's head:
For constant faith is made a drudge,
But when requiting love is judge.   50

20 · (LXVI)

Caelica, you (whose requests commandments be)
Advise me to delight my mind with books,
The glass where art doth to posterity
Show nature naked unto him that looks,
Enriching us, short'ning the ways of wit,
Which with experience else dear buyeth it.

Caelica, if I obey not, but dispute,
Think it is darkness which seeks out a light
And to presumption do not it impute,
If I forsake this way of infinite;   10
Books be of men, men but in clouds do see,
Of whose embracements Centaurs gotten be.

I have for books, above my head the skies,
Under me, earth; about me air and sea;
The truth for light, and reason for mine eyes,
Honour for guide, and nature for my way.
With change of times, laws, humours, manners, right;
Each in their diverse workings infinite.

Which powers from that we feel, conceive, or do,
Raise in our senses, thorough joys or smarts,   20
All forms the good or ill can bring us to,
More lively far, than can dead books or arts,
Which at the second hand deliver forth
Of few men's heads, strange rules for all men's worth.

False antidotes for vicious ignorance,
Whose causes are within, and so their cure,
Error corrupting nature, not mischance,
For how can that be wise which is not pure?
So that man being but mere hypocrisy,
What can his arts but beams of folly be?   30

Let him then first set straight his inward sprite,
That his affections in the serving rooms,
May follow reason, not confound her light,
And make her subject to inferior dooms;
For till the inward moulds be truly placed,
All is made crooked that in them we cast.

But when the heart, eyes, light grow pure together,
And so vice in the way to be forgot,
Which threw man from creation, who knows whither?
Then this strange building which the flesh knows not,   40
Revives a new-formed image in man's mind,
Where arts revealed are miracles defined.

What then need half-fast helps of erring wit,
Methods, or books of vain humanity?
Which dazzle truth, by representing it,
And so entail clouds to posterity,

Since outward wisdom springs from truth within,
Which all men feel, or hear, before they sin.

21 · (LXIX)

When all this All doth pass from age to age,
And revolution in a circle turn,
Then heavenly justice doth appear like rage,
The caves do roar, the very seas do burn,
Glory grows dark, the sun becomes a night,
And makes this great world feel a greater might.

When love doth change his seat from heart to heart,
And worth about the wheel of fortune goes,
Grace is diseased, desert seems overthwart,
Vows are forlorn, and truth doth credit lose,   10
Chance then gives law, desire must be wise,
And look more ways than one, or lose her eyes.

My age of joy is past, of woe begun,
Absence my presence is, strangeness my grace,
With them that walk against me, is my sun:
The wheel is turned, I hold the lowest place.
What can be good to me since my love is,
To do me harm, content to do amiss?

22 · (LXXI)

Love, I did send you forth enamelled fair
With hope, and gave you seisin and livery
Of Beauty's sky, which you did claim as heir,
By object's and desire's affinity.

And do you now return lean with despair?
Wounded with rivals' war, scorchèd with jealousy?
Hence changeling; love doth no such colours wear:
Find sureties, or at honour's sessions die.

Sir, know me for your own; I only bear
Faith's ensign, which is shame and misery;　　　　10
My paradise and Adam's divers were:
His fall was knowledge, mine simplicity.

What shall I do, sir? do me prentice bind,
To knowledge, honour, fame or honesty;
Let me no longer follow womenkind,
Where change doth use all shapes of tyranny;
And I no more will stir this earthly dust,
Wherein I lose my name, to take on lust.

23 · (LXXIV)

In the window of a grange,
Whence men's prospects cannot range
Over groves, and flowers growing,
Nature's wealth, and pleasure showing;
But on graves where shepherds lie,
That by love or sickness die;
In that window saw I sit,
Caelica adorning it,
Sadly clad for sorrow's glory,
Making joy glad to be sorry:　　　　　　　10
Showing sorrow in such fashion,
As truth seemed in love with passion,
Such a sweet enamel giveth
Love restrained, that constant liveth.
Absence, that bred all this pain,
Presence healed not straight again;
Eyes from dark to sudden light,
See not straight, nor can delight.
Where the heart revives from death,
Groans do first send forth a breath:　　　　20
So, first looks did looks beget,
One sigh did another fet,
Hearts within their breast did quake,
While thoughts to each other spake.

Philocel entrancèd stood,
Racked, and joyèd with his good,
His eyes on her eyes were fixed,
Where both true love and shame were mixed:
In her eyes he pity saw,
His love did to pity draw: 30
But love found when it came there,
Pity was transformed to fear:
Then he thought that in her face
He saw love, and promised grace.
Love calls his love to appear,
But as soon as it came near,
Her love to her bosom fled,
Under honour's burdens dead.
Honour in love's stead took place,
To grace shame with love's disgrace;   40
But like drops thrown on the fire,
Shame's restraints enflamed desire:
Desire looks, and in her eyes,
The image of itself espies,
Whence he takes self-pity's motions
To be Cynthia's own devotions;
And resolves fear is a liar,
Thinking she bids speak desire;
But true love that fears and dare
Offend itself with pleasing care,   50
So divers ways his heart doth move,
That his tongue cannot speak of love.
Only in himself he says,
How fatal are blind Cupid's ways,
Where Endymion's poor hope is,
That while love sleeps, the heavens kiss.
But silent love is simple wooing,
Even destiny would have us doing.
Boldness never yet was chidden,
Till by love it be forbidden.   60
Myra leaves him and knows best,
What shall become of all the rest.

24 · (LXXVII)

The heathen gods finite in power, wit, birth,
Yet worshippèd for their good deeds to men,
At first kept stations between heaven and earth,
Alike just to the castle and the den;
Creation, merit, nature duly weighed,
And yet, in show, no rule but will obeyed.

Till time, and selfness, which turn worth to arts,
Love into compliments, and things to thought,
Found out new circles to enthrall men's hearts
By laws; wherein while thrones seem overwrought,   10
Power finely hath surprised this faith of man,
And taxed his freedom at more than he can.

For to the sceptres, judges laws reserve
As well the practic, as expounding sense,
From which no innocence can painless swerve,
They being engines of omnipotence:
With equal shows, then is not humble man
Here finely taxed at much more than he can?

Our modern tyrants, by more gross ascent,
Although they found distinction in the state   20
Of church, law, custom, people's government,
Mediums (at least) to give excess a rate,
Yet fatally have tried to change this frame,
And make will law, man's wholesome laws but name.

For when power once hath trod this path of might,
And found how place advantageously extended
Wanes, or counfoundeth all inferiors' right
With thin lines hardly seen, but never ended;
It straight drowns in this gulf of vast affections,
Faith, truth, worth, law, all popular protections.   30

25 · (LXXVIII)

The little hearts, where light-winged passion reigns,
Move easily upward, as all frailties do;
Like straws to jet, these follow princes' veins,
And so, by pleasing, do corrupt them too.
Whence as their raising proves kings can create,
So states prove sick, where toys bear staple-rate.

Like atomi they neither rest, nor stand,
Nor can erect; because they nothing be
But baby-thoughts, fed with time-present's hand,
Slaves, and yet darlings of authority: 10
Echoes of wrong; shadows of princes' might;
Which, glow-worm-like, by shining show 'tis night.

Curious of fame, as foul is to be fair;
Caring to seem that which they would not be;
Wherein chance helps, since praise is power's heir,
Honour the creature of authority:
So as borne high, in giddy orbs of grace,
These pictures are, which are indeed but place.

And as the bird in hand, with freedom lost,
Serves for a stale, his fellows to betray: 20
So do these darlings raised at princes' cost
Tempt man to throw his liberty away;
And sacrifice law, church, all real things
To soar, not in his own, but eagle's wings.

Whereby, like Aesop's dog, men lose their meat,
To bite at glorious shadows, which they see;
And let fall those strengths which make all states great
By free truths changed to servile flattery.
Whence, while men gaze upon this blazing star,
Made slaves, not subjects, they to tyrants are.   30

26 · (LXXXI)

Under a throne I saw a virgin sit,
The red and white rose quartered in her face;
Star of the north, and for true guards to it,
Princes, church, states, all pointing out her grace.
The homage done her was not born of wit:
Wisdom admired, zeal took ambition's place,
State in her eyes taught order how to fit,
And fix confusion's unobserving race.
Fortune can here claim nothing truly great,
But that this princely creature is her seat.   10

27 · (LXXXIV)

Farewell sweet boy, complain not of my truth;
Thy mother loved thee not with more devotion;
For to thy boy's play I gave all my youth,
Young master, I did hope for your promotion.
While some sought honours, princes' thoughts observing,
Many wooed fame, the child of pain and anguish,
Others judged inward good a chief deserving,
I in thy wanton visions joyed to languish.
I bowed not to thy image for succession,
Nor bound thy bow to shoot reformèd kindness,   10
Thy plays of hope and fear were my confession,
The spectacles to my life was thy blindness;
But Cupid now farewell, I will go play me
With thoughts that please me less, and less betray me.

28 · (LXXXV)

Love is the peace, whereto all thoughts do strive,
Done and begun with all our powers in one:
The first and last in us that is alive,
End of the good, and therewith pleased alone.

Perfection's spirit, goddess of the mind,
Passèd through hope, desire, grief and fear,
A simple goodness in the flesh refined,
Which of the joys to come doth witness bear.
Constant, because it sees no cause to vary,
A quintessence of passions overthrown,   10
Raised above all that change of objects carry,
A nature by no other nature known:
For glory's of eternity a frame,
That by all bodies else obscures her name.

29 · (LXXXVI)

The earth with thunder torn, with fire blasted,
With waters drowned, with windy palsy shaken
Cannot for this with heaven be distasted,
Since thunder, rain and winds from earth are taken:
Man torn with love, with inward furies blasted,
Drowned with despair, with fleshly lustings shaken,
Cannot for this with heaven be distasted,
Love, fury, lustings out of man are taken.
Then man, endure thyself, those clouds will vanish;
Life is a top which whipping sorrow driveth;   10
Wisdom must bear what our flesh cannot banish,
The humble lead, the stubborn bootless striveth:
Or man, foresake thyself, to heaven turn thee,
Her flames enlighten nature, never burn thee.

30 · (LXXXVII)

Whenas man's life, the light of human lust,
In socket of his earthly lantern burns,
That all this glory unto ashes must,
And generation to corruption turns;
Then fond desires that only fear their end,
Do vainly wish for life, but to amend.

But when this life is from the body fled,
To see itself in that eternal glass
Where time doth end and thoughts accuse the dead,
Where all to come, is one with all that was;   10
Then living men ask how he left his breath,
That while he livèd never thought of death.

31 · (LXXXVIII)

Man, dream no more of curious mysteries,
As what was here before the world was made,
The first man's life, the state of Paradise,
Where heaven is or hell's eternal shade:
For God's works are like him, all infinite,
And curious search but crafty sin's delight.

The flood that did and dreadful fire that shall
Drown and burn up the malice of the earth,
The divers tongues, and Babylon's downfall,
Are nothing to the man's renewèd birth: 10
First let the Law plough up thy wicked heart,
That Christ may come, and all these types depart.

When thou hast swept the house that all is clear,
When thou the dust hast shaken from thy feet,
When God's all-might doth in thy flesh appear,
Then seas with streams above thy sky do meet:
For goodness only doth God comprehend,
Knows what was first and what shall be the end.

32 · (LXXXIX)

The Manicheans did no idols make
Without themselves, nor worship gods of wood,
Yet idols did in their ideas take,
And figured Christ as on the cross he stood,
Thus did they when they earnestly did pray,
Till clearer faith this idol took away.

We seem more inwardly to know the Son,
And see our own salvation in his blood;
When this is said, we think the work is done,
And with the Father hold our portion good: 10
As if true life within these words were laid,
For him that in life, never words obeyed.

If this be safe, it is a pleasant way,
The cross of Christ is very easily borne:
But six days' labour makes the sabbath day,
The flesh is dead before grace can be born.
The heart must first bear witness with the book,
The earth must burn, ere we for Christ can look.

33 · (XCI)

Rewards of earth, nobility and fame,
To senses glory, and to conscience woe,
How little be you, for so great a name?
Yet less is he with men that thinks you so.
For earthly power, that stands by fleshly wit,
Hath banished that truth which should govern it.

Nobility, power's golden fetter is,
Wherewith wise kings subjection do adorn,
To make men think her heavy yoke, a bliss,
Because it makes him more than he was born;   10
Yet still a slave, dimmed by mists of a crown,
Lest he should see, what raiseth, what pulls down.

Fame, that is but good words of evil deeds,
Begotten by the harm we have or do,
Greatest far off, least ever where it breeds,
We both with dangers and disquiet woo.
And in our flesh (the vanity's false glass)
We thus deceived adore these calves of brass.

34 · (XCIV)

Men, that delight to multiply desire,
Like tellers are that take coin but to pay,
Still tempted to be false, with little hire,
Black hands except, which they would have away:
For, where power wisely audits her estate,
The Exchequer men's best recompence is hate.

The little maid that weareth out the day
To gather flowers, still covetous of more,
At night when she with her desire would play,
And let her pleasure wanton in her store,   10
Discerns the first laid underneath the last,
Withered, and so is all that we have past:

Fix then on good desire, and if you find
Ambitious dreams or fears of overthwart,
Changes, temptations, blooms of earthly mind,
Yet wave not, since each change hath change of smart.
For lest man should think flesh a seat of bliss,
God works that his joy mixed with sorrow is.

35 · (XCVII)

Eternal truth, almighty, infinite,
Only exilèd from man's fleshly heart,
Where ignorance and disobedience fight,
In hell and sin, which shall have greatest part:
    When thy sweet mercy opens forth the light
Of Grace, which giveth eyes unto the blind,
And with the law even ploughest up our sprite
To faith wherein flesh may salvation find;
    Thou bidst us pray, and we do pray to thee,
But as to power and God without us placed,   10
Thinking a wish may wear out vanity,
Or habits be by miracles defaced.
    One thought to God we give, the rest to sin,
Quickly unbent is all desire of good,

True words pass out, but have no being within,
We pray to Christ, yet help to shed his blood;
   For while we say Believe, and feel it not,
Promise amends, and yet despair in it,
Hear Sodom judged, and go not out with Lot,
Make law and gospel riddles of the wit: 20
   We with the Jews even Christ still crucify,
   As not yet come to our impiety.

36 · (XCVIII)

Wrapt up, O Lord, in man's degeneration,
The glories of thy truth, thy joys eternal,
Reflect upon my soul dark desolation,
And ugly prospects o'er the spirits infernal.
Lord, I have sinned, and mine iniquity
Deserves this hell; yet Lord deliver me.

Thy power and mercy never comprehended,
Rest lively imaged in my conscience wounded;
Mercy to grace, and power to fear extended,
Both infinite, and I in both confounded;   10
Lord, I have sinned, and mine iniquity,
Deserves this hell, yet Lord deliver me.

If from this depth of sin, this hellish grave,
And fatal absence from my Saviour's glory,
I could implore his mercy, who can save,
And for my sins, not pains of sin, be sorry;
Lord, from this horror of iniquity
And hellish grave, thou wouldst deliver me.

37 · (XCIX)

Down in the depth of mine iniquity,
That ugly centre of infernal spirits
Where each sin feels her own deformity
In these peculiar torments she inherits,

Deprived of human graces and divine,
Even there appears this saving God of mine.

And in this fatal mirror of transgression
Shows man, as fruit of his degeneration,
The error's ugly infinite impression,
Which bears the faithless down to desperation;   10
Deprived of human graces and divine,
Even there appears this saving God of mine;

In power and truth, almighty and eternal,
Which on the sin reflects strange desolation,
With glory scourging all the spirits infernal,
And uncreated hell with unprivation;
Deprived of human graces, not divine,
Even there appears this saving God of mine.

For on this spiritual cross condemnèd lying,
To pains infernal by eternal doom,   20
I see my Saviour for the same sins dying,
And from that hell I feared, to free me, come;
Deprived of human graces, not divine,
Thus hath his death raised up this soul of mine.

38 · (CVIII)

What is the cause, why states that war and win
Have honour, and breed men of better fame,
Than states in peace, since war and conquest sin
In blood, wrong liberty, all trades of shame?
Force framing instruments, which it must use,
Proud in excess, and glory to abuse.

The reason is, Peace is a quiet nurse
Of idleness, and idleness the field
Where wit and power change all seeds to the worse,
By narrow self-will upon which they build;   10
And thence bring forth captived inconstant ends,
Neither to princes, nor to people friends.

Besides, the sins of peace on subjects feed,
And thence wound power which, for it all things can,
With wrong to one despairs in many breed,
For while laws' oaths, power's creditors to man,
Make humble subjects dream of native right,
Man's faith abused adds courage to despite.

Where conquest works by strength and stirs up fame,
A glorious echo, pleasing doom of pain,   20
Which in the sleep of death yet keeps a name,
And makes detracting loss speak ill in vain.

For to great actions time so friendly is,
As o'er the means (albeit the means be ill)
It casts forgetfulness; veils things amiss,
With power and honour to encourage will.

Besides, things hard a reputation bear;
To die resolved, though guilty, wonder breeds;
Yet what strength those be which can blot out fear,
And to self-ruin joyfully proceeds,   30
Ask them that from the ashes of this fire,
With new lives still to such new flames aspire.

39 · (CIX)

Sion lies waste, and thy Jerusalem,
O Lord, is fall'n to utter desolation,
Against thy prophets and thy holy men,
The sin hath wrought a fatal combination,
Prophaned thy name, thy worship overthrown,
And made thee, living Lord, a God unknown.

Thy powerful laws, thy wonders of creation,
Thy word incarnate, glorious heaven, dark hell,
Lie shadowed under man's degeneration,
Thy Christ still crucified for doing well.   10
Impiety, O Lord, sits on thy throne,
Which makes thee, living light, a God unknown.

Man's superstition hath thy truths entombed,
His atheism again her pomps defaceth,
That sensual unsatiable vast womb
Of thy seen church, thy unseen church disgraceth;
There lives no truth with them that seem thine own,
Which makes thee, living Lord, a God unknown.

Yet unto thee, Lord (mirror of transgression)
We who for earthly idols have forsaken   20
Thy heavenly image (sinless pure impression)
And so in nets of vanity lie taken,
All desolate implore that to thine own,
Lord, thou no longer live a God unknown.

Yet, Lord, let Israel's plagues not be eternal,
Nor sin for ever cloud thy sacred mountains,
Nor with false flames spiritual but infernal,
Dry up thy mercy's ever springing fountains.
Rather sweet Jesus, fill up time and come,
To yield the sin her everlasting doom.   30

A TREATISE OF MONARCHY

This is a long poem, in fifteen sections, devoted to an analysis of the principles and practice of government. Greville finishes by arguing the superiority of a monarchic system to government by either aristocracy or democracy.

Stanzas 27–33
The common frailty of Kings and subjects

Let each then know by equal estimation,
That in this frail freehold of flesh and blood,
Nature itself declines unto privation,
As mixed of real ill and seeming good;
And where man's best estate is such a strife,
Can order there be permanent in life?

Now if considered simply man be such,
Cast him into a throne, or subject's mould,
The function cannot take away this touch,
Since neither what he ought, or can, or would;   10
Both king and man perplexèd are in state,
Improve their ends, and set no other rate.

In which imperfect temper, expectation
Proves unto each a perverse enemy;
While power with sovereign partial contemplation
Aims at ideas of authority
More absolute than God himself requires,
Who of us only what he gives, desires.

Again, while people do expect from kings
Such a protecting popularity   20
As gives, forgives, intends no other things
But in a crown, a common slave to be,
This over-valuing each estate too far
Makes both full of misprision, as they are.

In judging other, then let either know,
As they are man, they are a mean creation

Betwixt the heaven above, and hell below,
No more deserving hate, than adoration;
Equal in some things are the great'st, and least:
One disproportion must not drown the rest.   30

The odds to be examined then is place,
What that doth challenge, what again it owes;
Not peising these in dainty scales of grace,
Where pure simplicity for wisdom goes;
Or vain ideas formed in the air,
To self-imagination only fair:

But in the world as thrones now moulded are
By chance, choice, practice, birth, or martial awe;
Where laws and custom do prescribe how far
Either the king, or subject ought to draw   40
These mutual ties of duty, love or fear
To such a strain, as every man may bear.

                    Stanzas 106–14
            Need for patience in bad times

How to prevent or stay those declinations,
And desperate diseases of estate,
As hard is as to change the inclinations
Of human nature in her love, or hate,
Which whosoever can make straight or true,
As well is able to create her new.

Hence falls it out, that as the wise physician
When he discovers death in the disease,
Reveals his patient's dangerous condition
And straight abandons what he cannot ease   10
Unto the ghostly physic of a might
Above all second causes infinite:

So many grave and great men of estate,
In such despairèd times, retire away,
And yield the stern of government to fate,

Foreseeing her remediless decay:
Loth in confusèd torrents of oppression
To perish, as if guilty of transgression.

Who then can wary Seneca reprove?
After he had observed his pupil's rage,
The brother poisoned (strange bewitching love)   20
The mother slain, of vice his patronage,
If he from bloody Nero did remove?
And as the pilots do, in tempests grown,
To fate give over art, and all their own.

But grant such spirits were to be excused,
As by oppression or necessity
Disgracèd live, restrainèd, or not used,
As part themselves of public misery;
Yet who are free, must labour and desire   30
To carry water to this common fire.

Have not some by equality of mind,
Even in the crossest course of evil times,
With passive goodness won against the wind?
So Priscus passed Domitian's torrid climes,
And, 'scaped from danger to the full of days,
Helping frail Rome with unoffending ways.

Was it true valour, or timidity,
That made stern Cato so impatient
Of his own life, and Caesar's victory?   40
Vanity it was, like smoke not permanent,
That wrought this weak work of strong destiny:
Where while he lost himself and Rome a friend,
He lost that glory which he made his end.

For since the most estates at first were founded
Upon the waving basis of confusion;
On what but fear can his discourse be grounded,
That in distress despairs a good conclusion?
With mysteries of which vicissitude,
Fate oftentimes doth human wit delude.   50

Again, who mark time's revolutions, find
The constant health of crowns doth not remain
In power of man, but in the powers divine,
Who fix, change, ruin, or build up again
According to the period, wane, or state
Of good or evil's seldom changing fate.

Stanzas 409–12
Importance of a strong navy

Therefore let thrones, whose states have seas to friend,
Study by trade to make their navies great,
As glorious engines when they will offend,
Magnificent theatres when they treat,
Bridges that will transport, and moving towers,
To carry in and out triumphing powers.

Under which safe, yet moving, policy
Did finite Athens make the infinite
Forces of Xerxes out of Greece to fly;
Lepanto likewise proves the Christian might   10
Able by sea to shake the Turkish power,
Where his land armies all the world devour.

England, this little, yet much envied isle,
By spreading fame and power many ways,
Admit the world at her land conquests smile,
Yet is her greatness reverenced by seas,
The ocean being to her both a wall
And engine to revenge her wrongs withal.

To which end kings must strive to add a spirit
Unto the mariner; in war and peace,   20
A minister of use and double merit,
Trained without charge to travel without cease;
Power hath no nobler nor yet surer way
Than that, by which both save and get they may.

A TREATY OF HUMAN LEARNING

In this treatise Greville sets himself first to demonstrate the fallibility and
inadequacy of the instruments of human learning—sense, imagination,
memory etc.—and argues that the results they produce must be fallacious
and misleading. In the second part of the treatise he enumerates the
various branches of learning, suggesting how some faults may be corrected
so as to produce a limited good in relation to wordly affairs. The stanzas
about poetry illuminate his attitude to his own work in this kind. He
tried to create a poetry which would be acceptable to 'solid judgements'
and combine the pleasing powers of ordered composition with state-
ments about the 'truth' of human situations, secular and spiritual, as he
understood it.

Stanzas 109–15
On poetry and music

... those words in every tongue are best,
Which do most properly express the thought;
For as of pictures which should manifest
The life, we say not that is fineliest wrought
Which fairest simply shows, but fair and like:
So words must sparks be of those fires they strike.

For the true art of eloquence indeed
Is not this craft of words, but forms of speech
Such as from living wisdoms do proceed;
Whose ends are not to flatter, or beseech,   10
Insinuate or persuade, but to declare
What things in nature good or evil are.

Poesie and music, arts of recreation,
Succeed, esteemed as idle men's profession,
Because their scope, being merely contentation,
Can move, but not remove or make impression
Really, either to enrich the wit,
Or, which is less, to mend our states by it.

This makes the solid judgements give them place
Only as pleasing sauce to dainty food;   20

Fine foils for jewels, or enamel's grace,
Cast upon things which in themselves are good;
Since, if the matter be in nature vile,
How can it be made precious by a style?

Yet in this life both these play noble parts;
The one, to outward church-rites if applied,
Helps to move thoughts, while God may touch the hearts
With goodness, wherein he is magnified:
And if to Mars we dedicate this art,
It raiseth passions which enlarge the mind,   30
And keeps down passions of the baser kind.

The other twin, if to describe or praise
Goodness, or God, she her ideas frame,
And like a maker, her creations raise
On lines of truth, it beautifies the same;
And while it seemeth only but to please,
Teacheth us order under pleasure's name,
Which in a glass shows nature how to fashion
Herself again, by balancing of passion.

Let therefore human wisdom use both these   40
As things not precious in their proper kind;
The one a harmony to move, and please,
If studied for itself, disease of mind:
The next (like nature) doth ideas raise,
Teaches and makes, but hath no power to bind:
Both ornaments to life and other arts,
Whiles they do serve, and not possess our hearts.

A TREATISE OF RELIGION

In this treatise Greville begins by claiming that the religious instinct is naturally present in all men. He goes on to give a psychological account of how this instinct is perverted through the 'self-love and fear' of corrupt nature so that, instead of leading to the truth, it creates false religions based on superstition and hypocrisy. True religion comes of grace and man's sinful nature may be redeemed by faith and obedience. In this extract he draws a forceful contrast between the religious outlook and the ways of the world.

Stanzas 105–11
God's truth and man's errors

This leads us to our Saviour, who no more
Doth ask than he enables us to do;
The rest he frees, and takes upon his score;
Faith and obedience only binds us to:
All other latitudes are flesh and devil,
To stain our knowledge and enlarge our evil.

Offer these truths to power, will she obey?
It prunes her pomp, perchance ploughs up that root;
It pride of tyrants' humours doth allay,
Makes God their lord, and casts them at his foot: 10
This truth they cannot waive, yet will not do,
And fear to know, because that binds them too.

Show these to arts, those riddles of the sin
Which error first creates, and then inherits;
This light consumes those mists they flourish in,
At once deprives their glory and their merits:
Those mortal forms, moulded in human error,
Dissolve themselves by looking in this mirror.

Show it to laws; God's law, their true foundation,
Proves how they build up earth and lose the heaven,   20
Give things eternal mortal limitation,

O'er-ruling him, from whom their rules were given:
God's laws are right, just, wise, and so would make us:
Man's captious, divers, false, and so they take us.

Show it the outward church; strange speculation
For that hypocrisy to see the life;
They that sell God for earthly estimation,
Are here divorced from that adulterous wife:
For this truth teacheth mankind to despise them,
While God more justly for his own denies them.   30

Offer these truths to flesh in general;
God in his power and truth they do confess,
But want of faith, that venom of their fall,
Despairs to undergo his righteousness:
They think God good and so his mercy trust;
Yet hold good life impossible to dust.

Only that little flock, God's own elect,
(Who living in the world, yet of it are not)
God is the wealth, will, empire they affect;
His law their wisdom, for the rest they care not: 40
Among all floods this ark is still preserved,
Storms of the world are for her own reserved.

AN INQUISITION UPON FAME AND HONOUR

As he does when he writes of human learning, Greville insists on the absolute worthlessness of fame and honour but also acknowledges that they may have some relative value in regulating the conduct of fallen man. In this extract he attacks the pride of the stoics and like-minded philosophers who claim that man has virtue enough within himself to be able to disdain the quest for fame and honour. For Greville, man has no power to make himself good. This is a work which only God can do. Until men recognise this and submit to God's law, they had better take advantage of any support, including the desire for fame and honour, which may be available to them, or their natures will degenerate even further.

Stanzas 20–29
Needful restraints on sinful human nature

Yet doth there rise from abstract contemplation,
A gilt or painted image in the brain,
Of human virtues, fame's disestimation,
Which, like an art, our nature so restrains,
As while the pride of action we suppress,
Man grows no better, and yet states grow less.

Hence they that by their words would gods become,
With pride of thought deprave the pride of deeds,
Upon the active cast a heavy doom,
And mar weak strengths, to multiply strong weeds:
While they conclude fame's trumpet, voice, and pen,
More fit for crafty states than worthy men.

For fame they still oppose even from those grounds
That prove as truly all things else as vain.
They give their virtues only human bounds,
And without God subvert to build again
Refined ideas, more than flesh can bear,
All foul within, yet speak as God were there.

10

Man's power to make himself good they maintain:
Conclude that fate is governed by the wise;   20
Affections they supplant and not restrain;
Within ourselves they seat felicities;
With things as vain, they vanity beat down,
And by self-ruin seek a Samson's crown.

Glory's dispraise, being thus with glory tainted,
Doth not as goodness, but as evils do
Shine, by informing others' beauties painted,
Where bashful truth veils neighbours' errors too;
All human pride is built on this foundation,
And art on art by this seeks estimation.   30

Without his God, man thus must wander ever,
See motes in others, in himself no beams,
Ill ruins good, and ill erecteth never,
Like drowning torrents, not transporting streams:
The vanity from nothing hath her being,
And makes that essence good, by disagreeing.

Yet from these grounds, if fame we overthrow,
We lose man's echo both of wrong and right;
Leave good and ill indifferent here below;
For human darkness, lacking human light,   40
Will easily cancel nature's fear of shame,
Which works but by intelligence with fame.

And cancel this, before God's truth be known;
Or known, but not believèd, and obeyed,
What seeming good rests in us of our own?
How is corruption from corrupting stayed?
The chain of virtues which the flesh doth boast
Being, since our fall, but names of natures lost.

In human commerce, then, let fame remain,
An outward mirror of the inward mind,   50
That what man yields, he may receive again,
And his ill-doing by ill hearing find:

For then, though power err, though laws be lame,
And conscience dead, yet ill avoids not shame.

But let us leave these stormy orbs of passion,
Where humours only balance one another,
Making our trophies of a mortal fashion,
And vanity of every act the mother;
For inward peace, being never wrought by fame,
Proves man's worth is no nature, but a name.   60

A TREATY OF WARS

Greville considers war from a number of points of view. War befits our
discordant natures and the fact that men demonstrate some qualities
such as diligence, courage and constancy, more amply in war than in
peace, only goes to show what affinity we have with the devil. In spite
of all that can be said against it, however, Greville acknowledges that in
the affairs of this world it is a useful and effective instrument of government. In the stanzas quoted, he sees war as being also an instrument of
God's policy by which He governs the growth and decline of worldly
powers. The vicissitudes of time indicate to man that the world itself is
not permanent but will at length fall into dissolution.

Stanzas 38–42.
War as an instrument of change

Needful it therefore is, and clearly true,
That all great empires, cities, seats of power,
Must rise and fall, wax old, and not renew,
Some by disease, that from without devour,
Others even by disorders in them bred,
Seen only, and discovered in the dead.

Among which are included secret hates,
Revolts, displeasure, discord, civil war;
All have their growing, and declining states,
Which with time, place, occasion bounded are: 10
So as all crowns now hope for that in vain,
Which Rome (the queen of crowns) could not attain.

This change by war enjoys her changing doom;
Irus grows rich, and Croesus must wax poor,
One from a king shall schoolmaster become,
And he made king, that wrought in potter's ore;
They who commanded erst must now obey;
And fame even grow infamous in a day.

That by vicissitude of these translations,
And change of place, corruption, and excess,   20

Craft overbuilding all degenerations,
Might be reducèd to the first address
Of nature's laws, and truth's simplicity;
These planting worth, and worth authority.

All which best root and spring in new foundations
Of states, or kingdoms; and again in age,
Or height of pride and power feel declinations;
Mortality is change's proper stage:
States have degrees, as human bodies have,
Spring, summer, autumn, winter and the grave.   30

ALAHAM

The play, *Alaham*, tells the violent story of the second son of a sultan of Ormus (at the mouth of the Persian Gulf) who, in order to seize the throne for himself, burns his father, brother and sister on the funeral pyre of another of his victims. His wife, whose lover he has killed, prepares for him a poisoned robe which he dons, and as he is suffering his death throes she adds to his torments by killing their child before his eyes. When Alaham is dead, she discovers that by mistake she has killed her lover's, not her husband's, child. She thereupon kills herself and the second child. The play owes a great deal to Seneca. There are choruses, long set speeches, the dialogue is formal, a nuntius is used to report action, and several episodes are adapted from Seneca's plays. *Agamemnon, Thyestes, Medea, Hercules Oetaeus* and *Hercules Furens* may all have contributed to the episodes. The interest of the story as Greville treats it is partly political. The old king was weak and by his weakness opened the way for Alaham's villainies: his incapacity was a political crime and results in disorder in the state. But the moral interest of the story is greater. Greville sees it as illustrating the workings of two dominating human impulses, lust for power and sexual lust; and his drama is a dynamic working out of the interplay of these. The two extracts consist of a discussion of human nature by a chorus of furies and part of Hala's last speech before she kills herself.

Chorus Secundus of Furies : Malice, Craft, Pride, Corrupt
Reason, Evil Spirits

Malice. Whence grows this fatal stay of our progression?
    Who have no friends are deaf to intercession.
    What can withstand our power? Our ends are evil;
    And so need fear no let from any devil.
Craft. We divers are in works though not in ends;
    And thereby every Fury finds some friends.
    Besides, we over-act, and therein foil
    The ruin of mankind wherein we toil.
Malice. Give me one instance: wherein do we fail?
Craft. In that we mankind unto fame entail.   10
Malice. That breaks religion's bounds, and makes him ours,
    By forming his God out of his own powers:

For if by conscience he did leave or take,
On that smooth face we could no wrinkle make.
Craft. Yet fame keeps outward order, and supports,
For shame and honour are strong human forts.
Whereas confusion is an engine fit
For us at once to swallow man with it.
Malice. Nay Craft! it is thy faint hypocrisy,
That mankind is so long protected by.   20
Thy often changes many times appease
Those Furies, which would else destroy at ease.
Craft. Fie Malice! It is you that us deceive,
Who but with violence only can bereave.
For which you find not many natures fit,
And so add little to our throne by it.
Where I pass thorough all the orbs of vice,
And form in each mould nature's prejudice.
The Christian church from me is not exempt;
Laws have by me both honour and contempt;   30
By me the war upholds her reputation;
And lust, which leaves no certain generation;
Envy, that hates all difference of degree;
And self-love, which hath no affinity;
Even you, without me, cannot prosper well:
I am the mould, and majesty of hell.
Pride. Craft, peace! thou cuttest every thread so thin,
As it destroys thy works ere they begin.
Thy cobwebs, like th'astrologer's thin line,
Fit for discourse, for use are over-fine.   40
Thy state is nothing else but change and fear,
Weeds that no fruit, but fading blossoms bear,
Clothed with pied colours of hypocrisy,
Which like to all is, yet can nothing be.
In you no soul finds stairs to rise withal,
Descent to craft, change, fear, being natural.
When I propound in gross, you minutes play,
Which is the cause our tragic works thus stay.
My wheels go on at once, thine restless pause;
Of little works, with much ado, the cause.   50
You even in Hala sometimes breed remorse,

At least a doubt that evil hath no force.
Thou makest Cain in undertaking slow,
Who must, to serve thy turn, like goodness show:
Those scenes still tedious are, those acts too long,
Where thy unresolute images be strong.
For while you fear your true tormentor, shame,
I swallow all at once, with honour's name.
Then glory not: since where thy links excel,
There we enlarge not, but contract our hell.   60
Corrupt Reason. Peace you base subalterns! and strive no more,
That but the carriers be of my rich store.
Perchance you think me th'object of you all,
And so no Fury, but the Furies' thrall:
Where I give form and stuff to make you worse,
And so become your lord, and not your nurse.
I break the banks of duty, honour, faith;
And subject am to no power, but to death.
Charge me; I grant, delays grow out of wit:
And are not all your false webs wrought by it?   70
To time I have respect, to person, place;
I cross myself to give my own acts grace,
I am base to you all, and so the chief,
Equal with truth, where I find good belief.
I bear the weight of fear, the rage of lust,
With self-love, envy, malice, left in trust.
I calm man's windy pride, distempered rage,
Giving to each a shape for every age,
Wrong I attire in purple robes of might,
That state may help it to be infinite.   80
And who is fitter here to rule you all,
Than I, that gave you being by my fall?
Know therefore all you shadow-loving spirits!
Who have no being but in man's demerits,
That infinite desires and finite power
At once, can never all mankind devour.
Though men be all ours and all we but one
The vice yet cannot build or stand alone,
Be it man's weakness that doth interrupt,
Or some power else that cannot be corrupt,   90

Or be there what there may be else above,
Which may and will maintain her own by love:
Yet have we scope enough to mar this state,
And to the ever being, what is late?
As men in your names image ugliness,
To check beloved children's wantonness
When they would have them do things, or forbear,
And call you when they know you are not there:
So I enamel your deformity,
Making all your excesses like to me.   100
And that you may believe this to be true,
We are not like: for what am I but you?

Evil spirits. Reason! You mar our mart, by coveting
Not to be equal with us, but our king,
For though you now like Roman augurs be,
Who, but your staff, have no true mystery,
Yet do you strive to rule, add, or diminish,
And idly so protract what we could finish.
Else how could Alaham or Hala stay
So long from making to our ends a way?   110
Lust's open face this age will easily bear,
And hope here current is to all, but fear.
Wrong needs no veil, where times do tyrannise
And what, but lack of heart, is then unwise?
Age hath descried those toys to be but name
Which in the world's youth did bear real fame;
Justice, religion, honour, humbleness,
Shadows, which not well mixed, make beauty less.
They help to smother not enlarge our fire,
By putting painted masks on man's desire,   120
And give time to unactive theory,
Which rage itself would not do, were it free.
So that we, Circe-like, change men to beasts,
Which beasts turn men again: too base a crest
For us, that would quite banish doing well
And so at once change heaven and earth, to hell.
In which course, who doth well observe each part,
Shall find mankind to have so strange a heart
As being all ill, yet no one ill serves

To work him to that mischief he deserves: 130
Fear, hope, desire, love, courage being mixed
So nicely in him, as none can be fixed.
Which is our glory: as for every state
To have a tempter fitted, and a fate.
A fear in great men still, to lose their might;
And in the mean, ambition infinite;
Truth in the witty held but as a notion;
Honour, the old man's god; the youth's, promotion.
All which opposing powers yet do agree
To work corruption in humanity. 140
Then on: this time is ours: what need we haste?
Since till time ends, our reign is sure to last.

ACT V, SCENE III, ll. 128–46

Hala. Come infant! Here is empire. Let us live.
This work is mine: Hell thanks, and envies me;
And lo! her spirits, before I come, I see. 130
Discord, sedition, rage, you furies all!
Possess again the state, where you began:
The woman you, 'tis we deceive the man.
Enter upon this large infernal womb,
Repay yourselves, this mould did make you all.
Why do you stay? Lead me the way: I come.
Flesh is too weak, it hath satiety;
Lust, intermittent here and fury, poor;
Rage hath respects, desires here weary be.
Leave man this mean: let us live in excess, 140
Where power is more, although the joys be less.
This child is none of mine: I had no part:
Bear him I did with loathing, not desire:
My womb perchance did yield, but not my heart.
With Alaham his father he must dwell:
I will go down, and change this ghost with hell.

MUSTAPHA

This play, like *Alaham*, is a non-theatrical, or closet, drama in the Senecan style and, also like *Alaham*, it tells a story of the east. The murder of Mustapha, which is the central episode, was an historical event which took place in 1553 and there were many versions of the story available for Greville to use.

Soliman the Magnificent, father of Mustapha, reigned from 1520–66 and was in many ways an admirable ruler. He was also a great conqueror who struck fear into Europe as his conquests spread westward. The play tells how suspicions are sown in his mind to induce him to believe that Mustapha, his son and heir, is plotting to kill and supplant him. Soliman is wracked by indecision, torn between natural affection for his son and fears for his own safety. The balance is finally tilted by Rossa, a freed bondwoman whom he has married and who has great influence over him. Rossa is Mustapha's stepmother and she wishes to have him removed so that her own son, Zanger, may inherit. Rossa's daughter, Camena, whose husband, Rosten, is an accomplice in Rossa's plots, tries to warn Mustapha of his danger but he refuses to save himself at the cost of disobeying his father and causing disturbances in the state. His death, in fact, nearly causes revolution, for his followers and the people rise in anger at Soliman's act. Achmat, Soliman's chief counsellor, debates with himself whether he should try to restrain the righteous anger of the people and decides that, whatever Soliman's guilt, the state must be preserved. Greville does not pursue the consequences of this decision.

Greville may have had several sources but his reading of the events is nevertheless individual and characteristic. Lust for power plays a large part here as it did in *Alaham* and the sexual passion of Soliman for Rossa is to be inferred, though it is treated much more explicitly in the sources than in the play itself; but essentially *Mustapha* turns on the contrast between those who live for this world alone and those who have a true sense of God and the life of the spirit. Rossa is totally obsessed by her ambitions and has no scruple even in murdering her own daughter in order to put her son on the throne. Mustapha, Soliman's eldest son, represents the rare soul who is totally free of attachment to the world and free of any kind of selfish ambition. The other characters are activated by varying degrees of vice and virtue between these extremes. Camena, Soliman's daughter by Rossa, and Achmat, Soliman's counsellor, are the best of them but they have commitments to the world and their acts can at best reflect only a tension between contrary duties; Heli, a priest,

agonises over his share of responsibility for Mustapha's murder but, since
he has no real spiritual resources, in the crisis he can only confess his lack
of faith in the religion he preaches and reveal his inner poverty. The
Beglerby is a time-server. Soliman himself is a man who asks God for
guidance, receives it in unambiguous terms, and rejects it because it
conflicts with his worldly self-interest. It is a feature common to all these
characters that they act deliberately and in full knowledge of the
implications of their situations. Tragic mistakes and ignorance play no
part in this tragedy. It is a drama of deliberate choices in which the good
are frustrated by the inevitable imperfections of human situations and
the wicked exercise their corrupt will and perverted intelligence but find
that disorder and destruction are produced by the efforts they make to
secure and enhance their positions. Only those who give no hostages to
the world, such as Mustapha, can really rise above it, and the world has
no place for them. Man's passions, his political nature, and his spiritual
states are all involved and put under scrutiny in this play and its language
often has reference to all three levels simultaneously.

THE CHARACTERS

Soliman (the Magnificent), emperor of Turkey
Rossa, his wife, and stepmother of Mustapha
Mustapha, Soliman's son
Camena, daughter of Soliman and Rossa
Rosten, Camena's husband
Zanger, son of Soliman and Rossa
Achmat, a counsellor
Beglerby, a high military officer
Heli, a priest

ACT I, SCENE I

Soliman, Rossa

Soliman. Rossa! Th'eternal wisdom doth not covet
　　Of man, his strength or reason but his love.
　　And not in vain: since love, of all the powers,
　　Is it which governs every thought of ours.
　　I speak by Mustapha: for as a father,
　　How often deemed I those light-judging praises

Of multitudes, whom my love taught to flatter,
Truth's oracles, and Mustapha's true stories?
So dearly nature bids our own be loved:
So ill a judge is love of things beloved.   10
But is contempt the fruit of parents' care?
Doth kindness lessen kings' authority,
Teaching our children pride, our vassals wit,
To subject us, that subject are to it?
This frailty in myself I conquer must,
And stay the false untimely hopes it works,
Threat'ning the father's ruin in the son:
Many with trust, with doubt, few are undone.
Sent for he is: nor shall the painted shows
Of fame or kindness longer seal mine eyes   20
For since he strives to undermine my crown,
I will as firmly watch to keep him down.
Rossa. Soliman my lord! The knowledge who was father
To Mustapha, made me (poor silly woman)
Think worth in blood had natural succession:
But now I see ambition's mixtures may
The gold of nature's elements allay.
His fame untimely born, strength strangely gathered,
Honour won with honouring, greatness with humbleness,
(A monarch's heir in courses popular),   30
Make me divine some strange aspiring mind;
Yet doubtful; for it might be art, or kind.
But look into him by his outward ways:
Persia, our old imbruèd enemy,
Treats of peace with the son, without the father:
A course in all estates to princes nice,
But here much more; where he that monarch is,
Must (like the sun) have no light shine, but his.
The offers: real crowns, or hopes of kingdoms.
What sudden knot hath bound up our divisions?   40
Made them that only feared our greater growing
Offer such projects for our greater growing?
'Tis true, that private thoughts may easily change:
But states, whose ways are time, occasion, seat,
Have other ends, than chance, in all they treat.

Yet be it all the world would us obey,
In monarchies which surfeit more than pine,
The king should judge: strength knows what strength can
   weld:
The best foundations else may over-build.
No, no: upon the pitch of high attempt   50
I see him stand, sporting with wrong and fear:
For law and duty both are captives there.
His hopes, the hopes of all; for all aspire.
His means, that proud, rebellious discontent,
Which scorns both governors and government.
Soliman! Fear is broke loose within me.
What will, or may, methinks already happens;
His power thus great, will fixed, occasion ready,
Shadows of ruin to my heart deliver.
Confusèd noise within my ears doth thunder   60
Of multitudes, that with obeying threaten.
Soliman! while fear to lose thee wisheth death,
My fear again to leave thee wisheth breath.
Soliman. Rossa! I scorn there should be cause of fears
  In one man's rage; for hard then were our state,
  That reins of all the world desire to bear:
  Yet thy disquiet shall increase my hate.
  Thy wishes vain to thee yet never were:
  For love and empire, both, alike take pleasure
  Part of themselves upon deserts to measure.   70
  And, but that all my joys have sorrow's image,
  I could say I take pride in thy affection:
  For power may be feared, empire adored;
  Rewards may make knees bow and self-love humble;
  But love is only that which princes covet,
  And for they have it least, they most do love it.
  Care therefore for thyself; I hold thee dear;
  And as for me!
  Though fortune be of glass and apt to break,
  Kings' life kept but in flesh, and easily pierced,   80
  Kings' crowns no higher than private arms may reach,
  Yet these all-daring spirits are rarely known
  That upon princes' graves dare raise a throne.

Rossa. Sir! few in number are time present's children;
  Where man ends, there ends discontentment's empire;
  Novelty in flesh hath always had a dwelling;
  Then tell me lord, what man would choose his room
  That must expect in wickedness a mean,
  Or else be sure to feel a fatal doom?
  Can that stay in the midst whose centre's lowest? 90
  Old age is nature's poverty and scorn;
  Desire's riches live in princes' children;
  Their youths are comets, within whose corruption
  Men prophecy new hopes of better fortunes.
  Ah sir! Corrupt occasion still preferreth
  The wisdom that for self-advantage erreth.
Soliman. Wisdom is not unto itself in debt
  That leaveth nothing but a God above it.
  Will he return from death unto the living?
Rossa. No sir! But much may hap before his death; 100
  Who thinking nothing worse and nothing after,
  Knows thought of wrong is death, if princes live;
  Where dead, all heirs their own good do forgive.
Soliman. I sent, he comes; and, come, is in my power.
Rossa. Before he comes, who knows your fatal hour?
  The wicked wrestle both with might and slight.
  While princes live, each man's life guardeth theirs,
  When they are dead, men's loves go with their fear.
  Slain by the way less grudge, more safety were.
Soliman. Wrong is not princely, and much less is fear. 110
Rossa. These glorious hazards tempt and hasten fate;
  They well become a man, but not a state.
Soliman. This fear in women shows a kindness too.
  And is for men to thank, but not to do.
Rossa. Is providence of no more use to power?
Soliman. Than to preserve the fame of power entire,
  Which often underminèd is by fear.
  I do suspect, yet is there nothing done.
  I lose my fame if I so kill my son.
  Though I yet know not he hath done amiss, 120
  I doubt, and heavy princes' doubting is.
  Though I resolve, I will not kill him there;

It mortal is if kings see cause to fear.
When Mustapha returns, my jealous care
Will very hardly danger oversee:
Order alone holds states in unity.

SCENE II

Beglerby, Soliman, Rossa

Beglerby. Fond man! distract with divers thoughts on foot,
  That rack'st thyself, and nature's peace do'st break;
  Judge not the gods above: it doth not boot,
  Nor do thou see that which thou dar'st not speak.
  Power hath great scope; she walks not in the ways
  Of private truth: virtues of common men
  Are not the same which shine in kings above,
  And do make fear bring forth the works of love.
  Admit that Mustapha not guilty be:
  Who by his prince will rise, his prince must please,   10
  And they that please judge with humility.
  Yonder they are, whose charge must be discharged.
  In Rossa's face behold desire speaketh,
  'He keeps the laws, that all laws for me breaketh.'
Soliman. Is Mustapha in health, and coming?
Beglerby. My lord! already come: for what can stay,
  Where love and duty both teach to obey?
Soliman In what strange balance are man's humours peised?
  Since each light change within us, or without,
  Turns fear to hope, and hope again to doubt.   20
  If thus it work in man, much more in thrones,
  Whose tender heights feel all thin airs that move,
  And work that change below they use above.
  For on the axis of our humours turn
  Church-rites and laws, subjects' desire and wit,
  All which, in all men, come and go with it.
  Rossa! A king ought therefore to suspect
  Fears, fearful counsels which incline to blood,
  Wherein, but truths, no influence is good.
  Else will inferior practice ever cast   30

Such glassy shadows upon all our errors
As he that sees not ruin, shall see terrors.
Power therefore should affect the people's stamp,
Whose good or ill thoughts ever prove to kings,
Like air, which either health or sickness brings.
Now Rossa! by these straight lines if we sound
The hollow depths of Rosten's mystery,
He will the canker of this state be found.
Long hath he waved betwixt my son and me,
Making succession sacred, whilst he felt   40
Practice could not divide the bark and tree:
His end being not to find or cherish truth,
But rather vices, where his art works ruth.
Long hath he weighed our humours with his ends,
To find which nature was the fittest mould
For him to bring to pass in what he would.
And though his power be on my old age built,
Yet that, as slow to ruin, he dislikes:
Guilt seeking shields for every blow it strikes.
Now in my son though active powers he find,   50
Yet what he cannot govern, gives offence;
From birth or worth still fearing competence.
He grounds this work on jealousy of kings,
Where hopeful goodnesses oft in successors
Seem not strengths, as they be, but strong oppressors.
And when this art could not procure his fall,
Nor shape our humours like Procrustes' bed,
Where all that fit him not are ruinèd:
Straight then he offers up unto my son
My life, my crown, and all that I have won.   60
Such slender props are princes' favourites,
Who like good fortune's children, love their mother
And never can be true to any other.
In these nets shall he then catch him and me,
And so this high and sovereign sceptre-power
Sink into slaves by my infirmity?
No, no: when princes, by defect of mind,
A proneness feel, to sink into their slaves,
Wherein they make their creatures their graves:

By nature have they not a phoenix-fire,   70
From their own ashes to revive again,
And in their children's honour live, and reign?
Then Rossa! judge: my love hath made us one,
And who can judge these humorists, but we,
Since hope and fear below lack eyes to see?
Mustapha is through misprision hither come,
Brought to the practice of this crafty slave,
Careless in which he makes the other's tomb:
His nets are laid; our thoughts for stales pitched down,
To catch ourselves in and, in us, the crown.   80
But nature's laws have conquered prince's doubts;
And between king and man what was begun,
Concludes betwixt a father and a son.

Rossa. Behold! these sandy hearts have no foundation:
Yet hence must I, with hazard, work my will,
That have to do with thought nor good, nor ill.
My lord! your doubts from arguments did rise
Of wanton pride, ambitious seeking love:
And can remissions be in nature wise,
While states upon the steep of danger move?   90
No: think what pregnant grounds of his ambition
Resolved you first his greatness was your danger:
And shall a father waive a king's suspicion?
Since mischief, whilst her head shows in a cloud,
In Pluto's kingdom doth her body shroud.

Soliman. Suspicion may enquire, but not conclude;
Both hope and fear do with excess delude.
Tell Beglerby! how did he welcome thee?
In your access what found you? pomp, or pride?
Was he reserved, or else did he descend?   100
Appeared I as his sovereign, or his friend?

Beglerby. His court was great; and that which adds to you
Is that all princes had their agents there
Confessing, in the son, the father's due:
And from them all the honour done him such,
As if none thought the world for him too much.
Yet I no sooner to his presence came,
But he paid all their homages to me,

The rest looked on, as when men wonders see.
Soliman. What was his cheer? did'st thou observe his eyes,   110
  When thou declared'st my will to have him come?
Beglerby. First, at your name he bowed in humble wise,
  The rest appeared to be a joyful doom.
  Only the Persian spake, it seems with care:
  'God make these favours good, for they be rare.'
Rossa. This is the glass which father looks not in:
  The workman hides, the instruments discover.
  See how it fits a king to be a lover!
  Sir! mark these words. Whence should their wonder grow?
  His scorn and grudge he worships and obeys: 120
  In him or for him, what strange works are these?
Soliman. Tell me his manner. How did he dispose
  His followers and affairs till his return?
  The news of war against our Persian foes,
  I am sure, made not his undertakers mourn
Beglerby. The Persian agent some distraction showed,
  All else their eyes to their sun rising turn.
Soliman. What's the discourse of court, and what the face?
  His carriage is it royally severe,
  Reserved like us, by attributes of place,   130
  Or popular, as power in people were?
  Shapes he his course to rule, or gain a state?
  Is our course changed or doth he imitate?
Beglerby. He winds not spirits up with power or fear,
  The ancient form he keeps where it is good.
  His projects reformation everywhere:
  His care to have diseases understood;
  Reverend unto your throne, more to your deeds,
  It is no imitation which exceeds.
Soliman. What doth he in our church or law reprove?   140
  What error in our discipline of war?
Beglerby. With zeal he doth adore the powers above;
  With zeal inferior duties paid him are:
  And for his ends on public centres move,
  His ends are served with everybody's love.
  His court, like yours, the image of a camp:
  In yours, your power; in his, himself the lamp.

He sees (men say) but only what he shows,
I mean examples both of power and love:
You see again what from within you grows,   150
Such humble fear as fearful power moves.
His camp, in rest and action both, content;
Assiduous order works this frame in either:
Your discipline now loose, now overbent,
Forced to use fear in both, contents in neither.
This freedom sir! makes them you two compare,
Of whom both he and they, but shadows are.

Soliman. What be his troops? an army, or a train?
Come they to dwell, or to go back again?

Beglerby. His will was to depart immediately,   160
With no train, but the Basha, priest, and I.
Your honour only ministered debate;
Princes (some thought) stood fast by keeping state:
His pomp gave lustre to your power, some said,
For princes should be gloriously obeyed.
At this gap entered love, and intercession,
The multitude all liberties approved,
The wise to give them way held it discretion,
Where it gave honour to your self above.
Thus to the coast number and order come,   170
Where Mustapha leaves all to bide your doom.

Soliman. Within the port, or where doth he attend?
What's the aspect between his own and ours?
Gains he or wanes he by approaching power?

Beglerby. His foot on land, straight to the church he goes.
Applause and wonder follow to that place.
Greater he, by your influence, still grows,
Your trophies upon him the people place.
Unto the state men prophesy progression,
And see your age, 'tis true, in your succession.   180
Your power and love, both, in his pomp appear;
For even the bashas next you I did meet
Hast'ning to honour him, whom you hold dear.
What greater triumph to a glorious father,
Than such a son for age to lean unto,
Whence declination may more forces gather,

And impotence retain ability to do?
Goodness exiling jealousy of state,
From him whose duty sets his power a rate.
Now by the way a paper up I took,   190
Spread by the mufti, as it should appear,
Foretelling with authority of book,
What those times wrapped in clouds, and these make clear.
Wherein these prophet-spirits did foreshow
The progress of this empire to the height;
Under what princes' humours it should grow,
Under whose weakness fall again by weight:
Inferring this: that where declining spirits
To govern mighty sceptres God ordains,
Order no basis finds, honour must fall: 200
Where man is nothing, place cannot do all.
Again where worth and wisdom sovereign be,
And he that's king of place, is king of men,
Change, chance, or ruin cannot enter then.
And such a king must sit upon this throne;
Unperfect times (they say) are fully run,
And this perfection present in your son.
Soliman. Change hath prepared her moulds for innovation.
I see inferior wheels of practice move,
Yet they prevail not on the powers above.   210
His worth rests constant, and yet works this motion,
They to him, for him, sacrifice at random
All which they have, and have not, in devotion.
He is the glass, in which their light affections
Come to behold what image they shall take:
If liberty they find, then anarchy they make.
On time, place, truth, these spirits never rest.
His worth, thus innocent, how can I fear?
Their thoughts, thus violent, can power digest?
Then government! thy hand must cut between   220
My fearful dangers, and his fearless praise.
In all states, power, which oppresseth spirits,
Imprisons nature, empire disinherits.
This throne grew not by delicate alliance,
Combining state with state, all states to laws,

Of idle princes and base subjects cause.
We grew by curious improving all,
Ourselves to people, people unto us;
Worth, through ourselves, in them we planted thus.
And shall I help to make succession less,   230
Blasting the births of nature and example,
In narrow fears of self-unworthiness?
No, no: the art of monarchy is more:
Princes must strength by such succession gather,
With future hopes all present smarts are eased:
Age hath a veil, and majesty is pleased.
Who makes, can mar. Honour, reward, and fear,
Are reins of power: the ends inherent there.
Rossa. Behold! I stand amazed: Sir! ease my heart.
A king less than a man! more than a god!   240
I know not where to stay, nor how to part.
God hath ordained that wickedness shall die:
Sir! who is guilty? Mustapha, or I?
Soliman. He now is in the hands of power, and time.
His danger is to come, and ours is past;
Let's see into what moulds our own are cast.
Rossa. Who will endure the sentence he may give,
Between you two? He must be king that lives.
Your grave preparèd is among your own:
Neighbours, church, people, soldiers, made the stage,   250
Where hope and youth shall ruin fear and age.
Most wretched I, raised to be overthrown.
If you will die, then am I lost in you;
And die you must, if you believe your own.
If he shall live, then am I proved untrue,
Hated by him whom you have placed above,
Lost unto you, and ruined by my love.
Ah confidence! thou glory of the ill!
How safely dost thou blinded power assail,
That having all, yet knows not what it will!   260
Soliman. Rossa! You move me; yet remove I not.
Man comprehends a man, but not a king.
I feel myself ('tis true) and I feel you;
How to itself can power then prove untrue?

Succession on the present never wins
But by the death of body, or of spirit:
All heirs by our mortality run in.
Let not misprision wound me in thy love:
Great inequality of worth you yield
To them, you think can on my ruins build.   270

Chorus Primus of Bashas or Cadis

Like as mixed humours, drawn up from the ground,
Are unto many forms and functions bound,
Partly out of their native property,
Partly the climes, through which their journeys be;
Some into meteors that amaze below;
Others to comets which forethreaten woe;
Some into hail-stones that afflict the earth;
Others to rain which hastens every birth;
Lightning and thunder only made of those,
Which the cold region's double heats enclose: 10
So is frail mankind, though in other fashion,
Raised and let fall with his own earthly passion;
Formèd, transformèd, and made instruments
In many shapes, to serve power's many bents:
Feeding superiors, even as vapours do,
Which spending themselves, scourge their parents too.
Some in mis-shapèd meteors terrifying
All constant spirits, under tyrants lying;
Others like winds, which Aeolus makes blow,
To breathe themselves out while they overthrow;   20
Some like sweet dews that nourish where they touch;
Like exhalations, some inflame too much;
Bondage, and ruin only wrought by those
That kings with servile flattery enclose,
Hatching, in double heats of power and will,
Thunder and lightning, to amaze, and kill.
Thus tyrants deal with people's liberty;
The nether region cannot long live free.
Thus tyrants deal with us of higher place,
As drawn up only to disperse disgrace.   30

Echoes of power, that pleasingly resound
Those heavy taxes wherewith princes wound.
Exhausters of frail mankind by our place,
To make them poor, and consequently base.
With colonies we eat the native down,
And, to increase the person, wane the crown.
With idle visions trafficking men's minds
To humble moderation, in all kinds:
Till under false styles of obedience,
We take from mankind all but suffering sense;   40
Yet even by these sails which for sceptres move,
We forcèd are with modest breath to prove,
Which way these people-tides will pass with ease;
Crowns wounding deeply, when they strive to please.
Whence, as we dare not blow them up to rage,
So again, if we quit this people-stage,
Thrones know not where to act those fancy-plays,
Which catch the lookers-on so many ways.
For we, like dews, drawn to be clouds above,
Straight grow with that attracting sun in love,   50
Which ever raiseth light things up to fall,
In crafty power creation natural.
Wrapped in which crown mists, men cannot discern
How dearly they her glittering tinctures earn,
Till, thorough glassy time, these cage-birds see,
That honour is the badge of tyranny.
    Laws the next pillars be with which we deal,
As sophistries of every common-weal;
Or rather nets, which people do ask leave,
That they, to catch their freedoms in, may weave,   60
And still add more unto the sultan's power,
By making their own frames themselves devour.
These Lesbian rules, with show of real grounds,
Giving right narrow, will transcendent bounds.
    The mufti, and their spiritual jurisdictions,
By course succeed these other guilt-inflictions:
Conscience annexing to our crescent-star
All freedoms, that in man's frail nature are;
By making doctrines large, strict, mild, severe,

As power intends to stir up hope, or fear: 70
Which heavenly shadow, with earth-centres fixed,
Rack men, by truth and untruths, strangely mixed;
And prove to thrones such a supporting cause,
As finely gives law to all other laws.
Thus like the wood that yields helves for the axe,
Upon itself to lay a heavy tax:
We silly bashas help power to confound,
With our own strength exhausting our own ground.
An art of tyranny; which works with men,
To make them beasts, and high-raised thrones their den, 80
Where they that mischief others, may retire
Safe with their prey, as lifting tyrants higher.
By which enthralling of ourselves, with others,
Prove we not both confusion's heirs, and mothers?
Far unlike Adam, putting civil names
Upon those errors which the whole world blames.
For if power ravin more than is her own,
People, we say, are chequers to a throne.
Again, if she to rise up, will pull down,
Creation, we say, still inheres the crown. 90
If good men chance to interrupt this way,
Too much in virtue oft there is, we say:
Since each inferior limb must from the head
Receive his standard and be balancèd.
If people grudge their freedom, thus made thrall,
Power is their body, they but shadows all.
If God himself, by law, or influence
Seems but to limit this omnipotence;
Even as in Christian courts of chancery,
Though land or titles cannot settled be, 100
Yet where the person dares to disobey,
Through him his title they imprison may:
So though with tyrants God transcendent be,
Yet plague they his for too much piety.
And by distinctions from the pulpit's doom,
Leave still for crown-impiety a room.
This is our office under tyranny,
Where power and passion only current be.

But where the better rules the greater part,
And reason only is the prince's art;   110
There, as in margins of great volumed books,
The little notes, whereon the reader looks,
Oft aid his over-pressèd memory,
Unto the author's sense where he would be:
So do true counsellors assist good kings,
And help their greatness on, with little things.
Honour, in chief, our oath is to uphold,
That by no traffic it be bought or sold.
Else look what brings that dainty throne-work down
Adds not, but still takes something from a crown.   120
Profit and her true mine, frugality,
Incident likewise to our office be:
As husbanding the sceptre's spreading right,
To stretch itself yet not grow infinite,
Or with prerogative to tyrannise,
Whose works prove oft more absolute than wise.
Not mastering laws, which freedom interrupts,
Nor moulding pulpits, which is to corrupt
And help change in; whose vanity still tends
To work immortal things to mortal ends.   130
But our part is to keep the justice free
As equal peising liberality;
Which both contents the people that receives,
And princely giver more enabled leaves.
Likewise with foreign states we keep respect
By diligence, which seldom finds neglect.
In treaties still concluding mutual good,
Since no one biased contract ever stood.
In compliments we strive to hold such measure,
That outward form consume not inward treasure.   140
For betwixt man and man, 'twixt king and kings,
Our place should offer well-digested things.
Else as those crudities which do remain
Within the body, all complexions stain:
So doth advantage between state and state,
Though finely got, yet prove unfortunate:
And oft disorder-like in government,

Leave even those that prosper, discontent.
  But is our great lord's character like these?
Are disproportioned humours made to please?   150
Can parricide, even unto nature treason,
Draw any true line from man's zenith, reason?
Then how can vice, in this confused estate,
Long 'scape the doom of never-sparing fate?
For as we see, when sickness deeply roots,
Meat, drink, and drugs alike do little boot;
Because all what should either nurse or cure
As mastered by diseases, grow impure:
So when excess (the malady of might)
Hath (dropsy-like) drowned all the styles of right,   160
Then doth obedience (else the food of power)
Help on that dropsy canker to devour.
In which crazed times, woe worth foreseeing wit,
Which mar itself may, cannot help with it.
For as those kings that conquer neighbour nations,
First by the sword make chaos of creations;
Then, spider-like, a curious netting spin,
Invisible, to catch inferiors in:
So when the art of powerful tyranny
Hath undermined man's native liberty;   170
Then, like lords absolute of words and deeds,
They soon change weeds to herbs, and herbs to weeds.
Which over-winding while the people fear,
Can tyrants hope of sanctuary there?
Or, when this fear hath tied men's minds together,
Proves this a storm, or constant winter-weather?
Again, when selfness hath men's hearts estranged,
Is not one sovereign soon to many changed?
Lastly, where absolute seems only wise,
Is not one envious there, in many eyes?   180
Disease thus grown, the crisis, and the doom,
Show princes must be ours, or we their tomb.
For as the ocean which is ever deep,
Under her smooth face doth in secret keep
The vast content of death's devouring womb,
Where those desires which venture find a tomb;

Aeolus, with sweet breath, making all things fair,
Till he hath bound hope prentice to his air;
Then adding more breath to that breath they spend,
Makes tide with tide, and wave with wave contend,   190
Enforcing men, for tax, to throw their goods
Into his merciless, enticing floods;
Where swallowing some in sight of those he spares,
Even they that prosper best must swarm with cares:
So doth vast power, at first, spread out her sleights
Of grace and honour; smooth bewitching baits;
And when men's lives, their goods, and liberty,
Are left in trust once with her tyranny;
Then, ocean-like, blown up with storms of passion,
Which, but excess, makes all seem out of fashion,   200
It takes advantage to devour the just,
Because to laws that limit thrones they trust;
Ruins the wise, whose eye discerns too much,
And thereby brings power's errors to the touch;
Discards the learnèd, for the difference
They make between the truth, and princes' sense;
Stains the religious, as if they withstood
Power's will, the stamp of all that's current good:
Yet saves it some, that they may witness bear,
Where power reigns, there worth must live in fear.   210
    Thus are we soothers, as all shadows be,
Sworn to the bodies of authority.
Thus do inferiors, catched with their own ends,
Pay double use for all the sceptre lends;
Not seeing, while man strives to stand by grace,
He offers nature's freedom up to place;
Whose true relation, between men, and might,
Assures us, thrones should not be infinite.
Lastly, thus do we suffer God to wane,
Under the humours of a sultan's reign.   220
And in the fatal ruin of his son,
Cut off our own lives, on a less thread spun.

ACT II, SCENE I

Achmat solus

Who, standing in the shade of humble valleys,
Looks up, and wonders at the state of hills;
When he with toil of weary limbs ascends,
And feels his spirits melt with Phoebus' glories,
Or sinews stark with Aeolus' bitter breathing,
Or thunder-blasts, which coming from the sky,
Do fall most heavy on the places high:
Then knows (though farther seen and farther seeing
From hills above than from the humble valleys)
They multiply in woes, that add in glories.   10
Who weary is of nature's quiet plains,
A mean estate, with poor and chaste desires;
Whose virtue longs for knees, bliss for opinion;
Who judges pleasure's paradise in purple;
Let him see me; no governor of castle,
No petty prince's choice, whose weak dominions
Make weak, unnoble counsels to be current:
But Basha unto Soliman; whose sceptre,
Nay servants, have dominion over princes:
Under whose feet the four forgotten monarchs,   20
The footstools lie of his eternal glory:
Even I thus raised, this Soliman's belovèd,
Thus carried up by fortune to be tempted,
Must, for my prince's sake, destroy succession,
Or suffer ruin to preserve succession.
Oh happy men! that know not, or else fear
This second slippery place of honour's steep,
Which we with envy get, and danger keep.
Unhappy state of ours! wherein we live,
Where doubts give laws, which never can forgive: 30
Where rage of kings not only ruins be,
But where their very love works misery.
For princes' humours are not like the glass,
Which in it shows what shapes without remain,
And with the body go and come again:

But like the wax, which first bears but his own,
Till it the seal in easy mould receive,
And by th'impression only then is known.
In this soft weakness Rossa prints her art,
And seeks to toss the crown from hand to hand;   40
Kings are not safe whom any understand.
First, of herself, she durst send Rosten forth
To murder Mustapha, his dearest son:
He found him only guarded with his worth,
Suspecting nothing, and yet nothing done.
Rosten is now returned: for wicked fear
Did even make him wickedness forbear.
A Beglerby goes since to call him hither;
The colour, war against the Persian king;
The truth, to suffer force of tyranny,   50
From his enforcèd father's jealousy.
Who utters this is to his prince a traitor:
Who keeps this, guilty is; his life is ruth,
And dying ever, lives denying truth.
Thus hath the fancy-law of power ordained,
That who betrays it most, is most esteemed:
Who saith it is betrayed, is traitor deemed.
I sworn am to my king and to his honour:
His humours? no: which they that follow most,
Wade in a sea wherein themselves are lost.   60
Yet Achmat stay! for who doth wrest kings' minds,
Wrestles his faith upon the stage of chance;
Where virtue, to the world by fortune known,
Is oft misjudged, because she's overthrown.
Nay Achmat stay not! for who truth environs
With circumstances of man's failing wit,
By fear, by hope, by love, by malice erreth;
Nature to nature's bankrupts he engageth:
And while none dare show kings they go amiss,
Even base obedience their corruption is.   70
    Then fear! dwell with the ill; truth is assured:
Opinion! be, and reign with fortune's princes.
Policy! go piece the faults of mortal kingdoms.
Death! threaten them that live to die for ever,

I first am nature's subject, then my prince's.
I will not serve to innocency's ruin.
Whose heaven is earth, let them believe in princes.
My God is not the God of subtle murder:
Soliman shall know the truth: I look no further.
    Behold! he comes like majesty confused;   80
Horror, revenge, rage lighten in his eyes.
All laws give place where power is joyned with these;
And he must go beyond that will appease.

ACT II, SCENE II

Soliman, Achmat

Soliman. Mercy, and love! you phrases popular,
    Which undermine and limit princes' thrones,
    Go, seek the regions of equality.
    Greatness must keep those arts by which it grew,
    And ever what it wills or fears make true.
Achmat. My lord! what moves these undermining words,
    Which showing fear in you, stir fear in us?
    Cruelty, and dissolution enter thus.
Soliman. Doth kings' restraint of wrath appear like fear?
    Shall our remissness suffer more than this?   10
    Can horror only, adoration bear?
    Behold, the world lays homage at my feet,
    To them by sword and fire I am known:
    Must kings that change this likeness lose their own?
    Two states I bear: his father and his king;
    These two, being relatives, have mutual bonds;
    Neglect in either, all in question brings.
    My son climbs up with wings of seeming merit,
    His course, applause, and mine, the scale of order;
    By dissolution, he builds up content,   20
    And I displease, by planting government.
    My age spends on the stock of honour won;
    Flesh hath her buds, her flowers, her fruit, her fall;
    Work hath his time, and rest is natural:
    His youth hath hope for right, and fame for end,

Time for a stage, for rival, expectation,
Ascending by the balance we descend.
Let youth affect goodwill, praise, reputation,
Fashion itself to times, or times to it,
Grow strong and rich in man's imagination: 30
But when her fame reflects scorn upon kings,
Her glory undermines, or else confounds
Of place, time, nature, all the reverend bounds.
These crooked shadows no straight bodies have;
Practice, ambition, pride, are here disguised.
And shall love be a chain, tied to my crown,
Either to help him up, or pull me down?
No, no: this father-language fits not kings,
Whose public, universal providence
Of things, not persons, always must have sense.   40
With justice I these misty doubts will clear.
And he that breaks divine, and human law,
Shall no protection out of either draw.
Achmat. Sir! where corrupted limbs art doth divide,
It hath no name of torment, but of cure:
Let many perish, so the state be sure.
Soliman. Then Achmat! Bid the eunuchs do their charge.
I wound myself in wounding of my son;
A king's estate hath of a father's won.
Advantageous ambition! hast thou learned   50
That present government still gives offences,
And long life in the best kings discontenteth?
That discontentment's hopes live in succession?
Well! False desires (which in false glasses show
That princes' thrones are like enchanted fires,
Mighty to see, and easy to pass over)
By Mustapha's example, learn to know;
No private thoughts can sound authority.
Achmat! I mean that Mustapha shall die.
Achmat. My lord! Good fortune doth me witness bear,   60
That my hopes need not stand upon succession,
Where life is poor in all but woe, and fear:
Then sir! doubt not my faith, though I withstand
This fearful counsel which you have in hand.

Soliman. Resolved I am. The form alone I doubt.
  Envy and murmur I desire to shun,
  With which yet great examples must be done.
Achmat. The form of proof precedes the form of death;
  Kings' honours and their safeties live in both:
  Against these to give counsel I am loth.   70
Soliman. Thought is with God an act: kings cannot see
  Th'intents of mischief but with jealousy.
Achmat. In what protection then lives innocence?
Soliman. Below the danger of omnipotence.
Achmat. Are thoughts and deeds confounded anywhere?
Soliman. In princes' lives, that may not suffer fear.
  Where place unequal equally is weighed,
  There power supreme is balanced, not obeyed.
Achmat. This is the way to make accusers proud,
  And feed up starvèd spite with guiltless blood.   80
Soliman. A just advantage unto kings allowed
  Whose safeties do include a common good.
Achmat. Sir! I confess, where one man ruleth all,
  There fear and care are secret ways of wit;
  Where all may rise, and only one must fall,
  There pride aspires, and power must master it:
  For worlds repine at those whom birth or chance,
  Above all men, and yet but men, advance.
  I know when easy hopes do nurse desire,
  The dead men only of the wise are trusted: 90
  And though crooked fear do seldom rightly measure,
  As thinking all things, but itself, dissembled:
  Yet Soliman! let fear awake kings' counsels,
  But fear not nature's laws, which seldom alter,
  Nor rare examples of iniquity,
  Which, but with age of time delivered be;
  Fear false stepmother's rage, woman's ambition;
  Whereof each age to other is a glass;
  Fear them that fear not, for desire, shame;
  Selling their faiths to bring their ends to pass.   100
  Establish Rossa's children for your heirs;
  Let Mustapha's hopes fall; translate his right:
  And when her proud ambitions glutted be,

Straight envy dies; fear will appear no more:
Nature takes on the shape it had before.

Soliman. Shall error 'scape by art? and shall a bare
Stepmother's name, in her that speaketh truth,
Disguise, and shadow parricide from blame?
Intents are seeds, and actions they include.
Princes, whose sceptres must be feared of many,   110
Are never safe that live in fear of any.

Achmat. Tyrants they are that punish out of fear,
States wiser than the truth decline, and wear.

Soliman. Thou art but one. The rest, in whom I trust,
Discern his fault, and urge me to be just.

Achmat. Though faction's strength be great, her sleight is more;
Her plots, and instruments inlaid with art:
Less care hath truth than hath the evil part.

Soliman. Traitor! Must I doubt all to credit thee?

Achmat. No less is truth, where kings deceived will be.   120

Soliman. The greater number holds the safest parts.

Achmat. That one is but the least of faction's arts.

Soliman. Thy counsel hazards all: their course but one.

Achmat. That painted hazard is but made the gate,
For ruin of your son to enter at.
Truth must the measure be to slave and king.

Soliman. Shall power then lose her odds in anything?

Achmat. God, even to himself, hath made a law.

Soliman. He doth for fame, what kings do but for awe.
What, but desert, makes those that praise accuse?   130

Achmat. The virtue they admire, and cannot use.

Soliman. Dare ought, but truth, assail a prince's child?

Achmat. On princes' frailties factions ever build.

Soliman. Speak plain, and free my soul from this disease,
That with the ruin of mine own would please.

Achmat. That which you will not feel, how can you see?
For in your love these works were all inweaved,
With which most worthy men are most deceived.

Soliman. What king or man loves fear, wrong, treachery?
These be the things that now in question be.   140

Achmat. Sir! where kings doubt, wisdom, and laws provide
Due trial, and restraint of liberty;

And unto caution their estate is tied:
But where kings' rage becomes superlative,
There people do forbear, but not forgive.
My lord! then stay: delays are wisdom, where
Time may more easy ways of safety show.
Self-murder is an ugly work of fear;
And little less is children's overthrow.
Mustapha is yours; more sir, even he   150
Is not, for whom you Mustapha o'erthrow.
Suspicions common to successions be;
Honour and fear together ever go.
Who must kill all they fear, fear all they see,
Nor subjects, sons, nor neighbourhood can bear:
So infinite the limits be of fear.
Soliman. Well Achmat! Stay. I strive to rest my thoughts.
Words rather stir, than quiet fixed impressions.
Kings' hearts must judge what subjects' hearts have wrought,
Not your calm heart unthreatened, and upright.   160
Such bees fetch honey from the self-same flower
Whence spiders draw their deep-envenomed power.
No, no; experience wounded is the school,
Where man learns piercing wisdom out of smart;
Innocence includes the serpent, not the fool.
The wager's great of being, or not being.
These crudities let me within digest;
My power shall take upon it all the rest.

ACT II, SCENE III

Camena, Soliman, Achmat

Camena. They that from youth do suck at fortune's breast,
And nurse their empty hearts with seeking higher,
Like dropsy-fed, their thirst doth never rest,
For still, by getting, they beget desire:
Till thoughts, like wood, while they maintain the flame
Of high desires, grow ashes in the same.
But virtue! those that can behold thy beauties,
Those that suck, from their youth, thy milk of goodness,

Their minds grow strong against the storms of fortune,
And stand, like rocks, in winter gusts unshaken,   10
Not with the blindness of desire mistaken.
O virtue, therefore! whose thrall I think fortune,
Thou who despisest not the sex of women,
Help me out of these riddles of my fortune,
Wherein (methinks) you with yourself do pose me:
Let fates go on: sweet virtue! do not lose me.
My mother and my husband have conspired,
For brother's good, the ruin of my brother:
My father by my mother is inspired,
For one child to seek ruin of another.   20
I that to help by nature am required,
While I do help, must needs still hurt a brother.
While I see who conspire, I seem conspired
Against a husband, father, and a mother.
Truth bids me run, by truth I am retired;
Shame leads me both the one way and the other.
In what a labyrinth is honour cast,
Drawn divers ways with sex, with time, with state?
In all which error's course is infinite,
By hope, by fear, by spite, by love, and hate;   30
And but one only way unto the right,
A thorny way: where pain must be the guide;
Danger the light; offence of power the praise:
Such are the golden hopes of iron days.
    Yet virtue I am thine, for thy sake grieved
(Since basest thoughts, for their ill-placed desires,
In shame, in danger, death, and torment glory)
That I cannot with more pains write thy story.
Chance therefore! if thou scornest those that scorn thee;
Fame! if thou hatest those that force thy trumpet   40
To sound aloud and yet despise thy sounding;
Laws! if you love not those that be examples
Of nature's laws, whence you are fall'n corrupted;
Conspire that I, against you all conspired,
Joined with tyrant virtue, as you call her,
That I, by your revenges may be named,
For virtue, to be ruined and defamed.

My mother oft and diversely I warned
What fortunes were upon such courses builded:
That fortune still must be with ill maintained,   50
Which at the first with any ill is gained.
I Rosten warned, that man's self-loving thought
Still creepeth to the rude embracing might
Of princes' grace: a lease of glories let,
Which shining burns; breeds serenes when 'tis set.
And by this creature of my mother's making,
This messenger, I Mustapha have warned,
That innocence is not enough to save,
Where good and greatness, fear and envy have.
Till now, in reverence I have foreborne   60
To ask, or to presume to guess or know
My father's thoughts, whereof he might think scorn:
For dreadful is that power that all may do;
Yet they, that all men fear, are fearful too.
Lo where he sits! Virtue! work thou in me,
That what thou seekest may accomplished be.
Soliman. Ah death! is not thy self sufficient anguish,
But thou must borrow fear, that threat'ning glass,
Which, while it goodness hides and mischief shows,
Doth lighten wit to honour's overthrows?   70
But hush: methinks away Camena steals:
Murder, belike, in me itself reveals.
Camena! whither now? why haste you from me?
Is it so strange a thing to be a father?
Or is it I that am so strange a father?
Camena. My lord! methought, nay, sure, I saw you busy:
Your child presumes, uncalled, that comes unto you.
Soliman. Who may presume with fathers, but their own,
Whom nature's law hath ever in protection,
And gilds in good belief of dear affection?   80
Camena. Nay, reverence, sir, so children's worth doth hide,
As of the fathers it is least espied.
Soliman. I think it's true: who know their children least,
Have greatest reason to esteem them best.
Camena. How so, my lord? Since love in knowledge lives,
Which unto strangers, therefore, no man gives.

Soliman. The life we gave them soon they do forget,
　While they think our lives do their fortunes let.
Camena. The tenderness of life it is so great,
　As any sign of death we hate too much;　　　　　　　90
　And unto parents, sons, perchance, are such.
　Yet nature meant her strongest unity
　'Twixt sons and fathers; making parents cause
　Unto the sons of their humanity,
　And children pledge of their eternity.
　Fathers should love this image in their sons.
Soliman. But streams back to their springs do never run.
Camena. Pardon, my lord! Doubt is succession's foe:
　Let not her mists poor children overthrow.
　Though streams from springs do seem to run away,　　100
　'Tis nature leads them to their mother sea.
Soliman. Doth nature teach them, in ambition's strife,
　To seek his death by whom they have their life?
Camena. Things easy, to desire impossible do seem:
　Why should fear make impossible seem easy?
Soliman. Monsters yet be; and being, are believed.
Camena. Incredible hath some inordinate progression:
　Blood, doctrine, age, corrupting liberty,
　Do all concur, where men such monsters be.
　Pardon me, sir, if duty do seem angry:　　　　　　110
　Affection must breathe out afflicted breath,
　Where imputation hath such easy faith.
Soliman. Mustapha is he that hath defiled his nest;
　The wrong the greater, for I loved him best.
　He hath devised that all at once should die,
　Rosten, and Rossa, Zanger, thou and I.
Camena. Fall none but angels suddenly to hell?
　Are kind and order grown precipitate?
　Did ever any other man, but he,
　In instant lose the use of doing well?　　　　　　120
　Sir! these be mists of greatness. Look again:
　For kings that, in their fearful icy state,
　Behold their children as their winding sheet,
　Do easily doubt; and what they doubt, they hate.
Soliman. Camena, thy sweet youth that knows no ill

Cannot believe thine elders, when they say
That good belief is great estates' decay.
Let it suffice that I, and Rossa too,
Are privy what your brother means to do.

Camena. Sir, pardon me, and nobly as a father   130
What I shall say, and say of holy mother,
Know I shall say it, but to right a brother.
My mother is your wife: duty in her
Is love: she loves; which not well governed bears
The evil angel of misgiving fears;
Whose many eyes, whilst but itself they see,
Still make the worst of possibility.
Out of this fear she Mustapha accuseth:
Unto this fear, perchance, she joins the love
Which doth in mothers for their children move.   140
Perchance, when fear hath shown her yours must fall,
In love she sees that hers must rise withal.
Sir, fear a frailty is, and may have grace,
And over-care of you cannot be blamed;
Care of our own in nature hath a place,
Passions are oft mistaken and mis-named,
Things simply good grow evil with mis-placing;
Though laws cut off and do not care to fashion,
Humanity of error hath compassion.
Yet God forbid, that either fear, or care,   150
Should ruin those that true and faultless are.

Soliman. Is it no fault, or fault I may forgive
For son to seek the father should not live?

Camena. Is it a fault, or fault for you to know,
My mother doubts a thing that is not so?
These ugly works of monstrous parricide,
Mark from what hearts they rise, and where they bide.
Violent, despaired, where honour broken is;
Fear lord; time death; where hope is misery,
Doubt having stopped all honest ways to bliss,   160
And custom shut the windows up of shame,
That craft may take upon her wisdom's name.
Compare now Mustapha with this despair:
Sweet youth, sure hopes, honour, a father's love,

No infamy to move, or banish fear,
Honour to stay, hazard to hasten fate:
Can horrors work in such a child's estate?
Besides, the Gods, whom kings should imitate,
Have placed you high to rule, not overthrow.
For us, not for your selves, is your estate: 170
Mercy must hand in hand with power go.
Your sceptre should not strike with arms of fear,
Which fathoms all men's imbecility,
And mischief doth, lest it should mischief bear.
As reason deals within with frailty,
Which kills not passions that rebellious are,
But adds, subtracts, keeps down ambitious spirits:
So must power form, not ruin instruments:
For flesh and blood, the means 'twixt heaven and hell,
Unto extremes extremely racked be;   180
Which kings in art of government should see.
Else they, which circle in themselves with death,
Poison the air, wherein they draw their breath.
Pardon my lord! Pity becomes my sex:
Grace with delay grows weak, and fury wise.
Remember Theseus' wish and Neptune's haste
Killed innocence, and left succession waste.
Soliman. If what were best for them that do offend
  Laws did enquire, the answer must be 'Grace'.
  If mercy be so large, where's justice' place?   190
Camena. Where love despairs, and where God's promise ends.
  For mercy is the highest reach of wit,
  A safety unto them that save with it:
  Born out of God, and unto human eyes,
  Like God, not seen, till fleshly passion dies.
Soliman. God may forgive, whose being and whose harms
  Are far removed from reach of fleshly arms:
  But if God equals or successors had,
  Even God of safe revenges would be glad.
Camena. While he is yet alive, he may be slain,   200
  But from the dead no flesh comes back again.
Soliman. While he remains alive, I live in fear.
Camena. Though he were dead, that doubt still living were.

Soliman. None hath the power to end what he begun.
Camena. The same occasion follows every son.
Soliman. Their greatness or their worth is not so much.
Camena. And shall the best be slain, for being such?
Soliman. Thy mother or thy brother are amiss:
   I am betrayed, and one of them it is.
Camena. My mother, if she errs, errs virtuously;   210
   And let her err, ere Mustapha should die.
   Kings for their safety must not blame mistrust,
   Nor for surmises sacrifice the just.
Soliman. Well, dear Camena, keep this secretly.
   I will be well advised before he die.
   Come Achmat. To the church, We will go pray
   God, to unfold this probability.
   Where power and wit so much offend him may.
   In this disease of spirits, the true appeal
   Is to that judge that every spirit knows,   220
   For we by error else may honour lose.
   His laws, the life, the innocence, the state
   Of son and father now in balance stand.
   Kings that have cause to fear, take leave to hate;
   Sons that aspire as eas'ly lift their hands.
   If I fall now, I give that scope to fate,
   Our equal gage being only nature's bands.
   Help comes alike to each of us too late,
   If aught between us and advantage stand.
   Yet she and you a strife within me move,   230
   And rest I will with counsel from above.

Chorus Secundus of Mahomedan Priests

If among Christians even the best divines
Conclude their church (though thrall to human might)
Yet to be such a fair mould as refines
And guides kings' power, else indefinite,
That it no tyrant or prophaner be,
Horrors too frequent in authority:

May not our conquering true church then assume
By grace and duty to link God to kings

And kings to man? which what else could presume?
Since might and number rule all other things.   10
Then crowns! what honour to our church is due
That fashions itself thus, to fashion you!

Laws we had none, but what our priests inspired.
Our right was less, for we had nought to claim.
To propagate itself the truth desired
And to that end, at all mankind did aim:
So that while souls we only sought to save,
They are with God, and we their empires have.

Ali, a prophet from our church divided
In outward forms, not lines of inward life,   20
Like witty schism we lovingly decided
With well-bent spirits in opinion's strife.
Europe in chief our prophets then withstood
With her three-mitred God of flesh and blood.

Her lettered Greece, that lottery of arts,
Since Mars forsook her subtle, never wise,
Proud of her new-made Gods in fleshly hearts,
As she of old was of her heathen lies,
We undertook with unity of mind,
And what their wits dispute, our swords did bind.   30

So that, ere her cross sects could danger see,
Their thrones, schools, mitres, idols were resigned
To us, new trophies of our monarchy.
Thus are the muses still by Mars refined,
And thus our church, by pulling others down,
I fear o'erbuilt itself, perchance the crown.

For till of late our church and prince were one,
No latitude left either to divide.
The word and sword endeavoured not alone,
But were, like mutual voice and echo tied   40
With one desire, jointly to move, speak, do,
As if fate's oracles, and actors too.

Now while the crown and priest-hood joinèd thus
In equal ends, though dignities distinct,
As man's soul to his body linkèd is:
Crowns, by this tincture of divine instinct,
So above nature raised the laws of might,
As made all errors of the world our right.

Vices, I grant, our martial course then had,
For spoil, blood, lust, were therein left too free,   50
As raising strong ideas in the bad,
Brave instruments of sovereignity.
Like thieves, at home our justice was severe,
In other princes' realms our freedoms were.

Great the seraglio was, I must confess,
Yet so as kindle did, not quench our spirits.
Our pleasures never made our natures less.
Venus was joined with Mars to stir up merits.
In right or wrong our course was not precise,
Nor is, in any state that multiplies;   60

Yet, to redeem this discipline of vice,
We added to the glory of our state,
Won honour by them, to the prejudice
Of strangers, conquering more than we did hate.
Our emulation was with crowns, not men.
Thus did our vices spread our empire then.

Where since, though we still spoil that Christian sect,
Which, by division fatal to their kind,
Friends, duties, enemies, and right neglect,
To keep up some self-humour in the wind: 70
Yet all we thus win, not by force but sleight,
Poised with our martial conquests, will lack weight.

For force, not right, our crescents bear in chief.
Camps and not courts are maps of our estate,
Where church, law, will, all discipline, in brief,
Established are to make worth fortunate.

We scorn those arts of peace, that civil tether,
Which in one bond tie craft and force together.

Of cell-bred sciences we chew no cud.
Our food and garments overload us not.   80
When one act withers, straight another buds.
Our rest is doing, good success our lot.
Our beasts are no more delicate than we.
This odds have Turks of Christianity.

Yet by our traffic with this dreaming nation,
Their conquered vice hath stained our conquering state,
And brought thin cobwebs into reputation,
Of tender subtlety; whose step-mother, Fate,
So inlays courage with ill-shadowing fear,
As makes it much more hard to do than bear.   90

And, as in circles, who breaks any part
That perfect form doth utterly confound,
Or as among the feignèd lines of art,
One only right is, all else crooked found:
So from our prophet's saws, when sultans stray,
In human wit power finds perplexèd way.

Hence, though we make no idols, yet we fashion
God as if from power's throne he took his being,
Our Alchoran as warrant unto passion,
Monarchs in all laws but their own will seeing.   100
He whom God chooseth out of doubt doth well:
What they that choose their God do, who can tell?

Again, when great states learn civility
Of petty kingdoms, learn they not to fall?
Nay, monarchies, when they declining be,
Brook they those virtues which they rose withal?
Had Mustapha been born in Selim's time,
What now is fearful, then had been sublime.

The Christian bondage is much more refined,
Though not in real things, in real names,   110

Laws, doctrine, discipline, being all assigned
To hold upright that witty man-built frame,
Where every limb, though in themselves distinct,
Yet finely are unto the sceptre linked.

An art by which man seems, but is not free,
Crowns keeping all their specious guiding reins
Fast in the hand of strong authority,
So to relax, or wind up passion's chains
As before humble people know their grief
Their states are used to look for no relief.   120

Yet if by parts we travail to compare
What differences 'twixt these two empires are:
We build no citadels, our strengths are men,
And hold retreat to be the loser's den.
They by their forts mow their own people down,
A way perchance to keep, not spread, a crown.
Of bondage we leave our succession free.
Office and action are our liberty.
They may inherit land: we hope for place.
They give the wealthy, we the active grace.   130
We hear the fault, and so demand that head
Which hath in martial duties been misled.
Their process is to answer and appear,
But under laws which hold the sceptre dear.
Our law is martial, sudden and severe,
For fact can rarely intricateness bear.
Their laws take life from sovereignity,
Thankless to which, power will not let them be.
So that the Mussulman sends home his head:
The Christian keeps his own, till he be dead.   140
Our trade is tax, comprising men and things:
And draw not they mankind's wealth under kings?
Soothing the tyrant, till by his excess,
Want makes the majesty of thrones grow less,
By taxing people's vice at such a rate
As, to fill up a sieve, exhausts a state.
Lastly, so shuffling trade, law, doctrine, will,

As no soul shall find peace in good or ill;
Both being traps alike used to entice
The weak and humble into prejudice.   150
Our sultans rule their charge by prophet's saws
And leave the mufti judge of all their laws.
The Christians take and change faith with their kings
Which under mitres oft the sceptre brings.
We make the church our sultan's instrument:
They with their kings will make their church content.
They wrangle with themselves and by dispute
In questions, think to make the one side mute;
If not, then sacrifice the weaker part,
As if, in thrones, blood were religion's art;   160
Forcing the will, which is to catch the wind,
As if man's nature were more than his mind.
We, in subduing Christians, conquer both,
And to lose use of either part are loth.
So that we suffer their fond zeal to pray
That it may well our conquering armies pay.
And where we are, there Christians fain would be,
If lack of power were not their modesty.
Thus do all great states safely manage things
Which danger seems to thrones of petty kings.   170
For though the sick have sense of every breath
And shun all what they feel, for fear of death,
Yet in strong states, those storms they feel give health
And by their purgings spoil infection's stealth;
A play of sun-motes, from man's small world come
Upon the great world to work heavy doom.
    For proof: behold in Soliman that fear
Which torrid zones of tyranny must bear.
For who hath lost man's nature in his passion
Can never see the world in better fashion,   180
Bur credit gives to limitless suspicion,
Which unto all vice giveth one condition,
Confusion's orb: where men may hate their own,
Nature and reason there being overthrown.
Hence go out mandates of conspiracy
'Gainst Mustapha, who must not guiltless be

In such a father's and a monarch's eyes
As will see nothing but destruction wise.
Hence Mustapha, from like dreams of the heart,
Sees his destruction wrought by tyrant's art,   190
And yet yields things to names, his right to passion,
Which misplaced duties help power to dis-fashion.
Nay, hence mankind, by crafty power oppressed,
Where it hath given part, still gives the rest;
And thinking thrones in all their practice true,
Dare not of their own creatures ask their due:
But rather, like mild earth with weeds o'ergrown,
Yields to be ploughed, manured and overthrown.
Lastly, thus sceptres fall with their own weight
When climbing power, once risen to her height,   200
Descends to make distinction in her lust
Which grants that absolute may be unjust,
And so subjects to censure what should reign,
Steps to bring power to people back again.
Whence I conclude: Mankind is both the form
And matter, wherewith tyrannies transform.
For power can neither see, work, or devise,
Without the people's hands, hearts, wit, and eyes:
So that were man not by himself oppressed
Kings would not, tyrants could not make him beast.   210

ACT III, SCENE I

Rossa, Rosten

Rossa. O wearisome obedience, wax to power!
    Shall I in vain be Mustapha's accuser?
    Shall any justice equal him and me?
    Is love so open-eared, my power so weak
    As aught against me to my lord dare speak?
    Sands shall be numbered first and motion fixed,
    The sea exchange her channel with the fire
    Before my will or reason stand in awe
    Of God or nature, common people's law.
Rosten. Rossa, whence grows this strange unquiet motion?   10

Govern your thoughts. What want you to content you,
That have the king of kings at your devotion?
Rossa. Content ? O poor estate of woman's wit!
The latitude of princes is desire
Which all it hath enjoyed still carries higher.
Say you the world is left to my devotion?
Who questioned am both in my state and fame,
Must lose my will, and cannot lose my shame;
For Mustapha, long since condemned to die,
Now lives again.   20
To boast of marriage then what ground have I ?
Rosten. Conclude not now: for thoughts that be offended
Are seldom with their present visions mended.
Rage sees too much, security too little;
Affections are, like glassy metal, brittle.
Rossa. Ah servile sex! must yokes our honour be,
To make our own loves our captivity?
No, Rossa, no. Look not in languished wit,
For none can stand on fortune's steep with it.
Think innocency harm, virtue dishonour,   30
Wound truth and overweigh the scale of right.
Sexes have ways apart. States have their fashions.
The virtues of authority are passions.
Rosten. Rossa, take heed.
Your honours, like kings' humours, brittle are,
Which, broken once, repaired can hardly be,
And these once stained, what is humanity?
Rossa, first judge your ends, and then your means.
You seek to undermine a prince's state,
Deep rooted in by time, power, reverence,   40
Established on succession fortunate
Of many Turks: from men that servile be,
Use having lost the use of liberty.
I understand a monarch's state too well,
To bid you purchase people's idle breath
That have no power of honour, life, or death.
These ways are wrong, uncertain, fearful too,
In absolutes, which all themselves will do.
But turn your eyes up to the will of one.

Know you must work a father from his son.   50
Rossa. This parent's dotage, as it weakness is,
    So works it with the vigour of disease
    Still undermining with the things that please.
    Upon this quick-sand what can be begun?
Rosten. Son's love with self-love must be overthrown.
    By force of nature's law there's nothing won.
    Strifes in the father's mind you must beget
    And him above his sweet affections bear,
    To take impressions both of hope and fear.
Rossa. Those silly natures apt to lovingness,   60
    Which ever must in others' power live,
    With doubt become more fond, with wrong more thrall.
    Fear here wants eyes, hate hath no sting at all.
Rosten. All these false strengths of native confidence
    With their excess have their inconstancy.
    The laws of kind, with tyrants, nothing be.
    Besides, dear Rossa, ills have such alliance
    As in what subject any one is grown
    The seeds of all, even in that one, are sown.
Rossa. This mass of passions who can deal withal?   70
    Too nice and subtle is inconstancy.
    Shall wrong fair-written still in patience be?
    Must my desire so many cautions have,
    And wait on those thoughts that have worshipped me?
    I cannot bear this mediocrity.
Rosten. Rossa, take heed, Extremes are not the means
    To change estates, either in good or ill.
    Therefore yield not, since that makes nature less,
    Nor yet use rage, which vainly driveth on
    The mind to working without instruments.   80
    Besides, it doth make partial our intents,
    Discredits truth, condemns indifferent things.
    But take upon you quiet providence,
    The prince's state, with his authority.
    Teach power to doubt, for doubt is her defence.
    Degrees of passions, as of spirits there be:
    Choose now for use and not for dignity.
    Love spreads the wit to play, but not to arm,

Hath many feet to walk an easy pace,
Slow to mistrust and never apt to harm.   90
But fear, of credit is within the mind,
Strengthened by nature with the strength of all,
In men and tyrants' states, both, natural.
The project of this fear must yet be made
The prince's safety, honour of the state.
Such glorious styles may easily overshade
The ways of spite, for treason is in hate.
Flattery straight speaks aloud in power's right,
Carrying things under names, truth under might.
Who dare distinguish in a tyranny,   100
Where fraud itself hath power's authority?
Who shall correct errors made for the king
But kings themselves? who, actors in their fears,
Most honour those that most suspicion bring.
Who there sees right, or dare use honour's name
Where both are sure of death and doubtful fame?
Then Rossa, plant you here. Accuse the son.
Although you fail his death, you need not doubt.
In tyrant's state never was man undone
By miscomplaints. Besides, what comes about   110
In earth but it hath lets and finds delays?
Yield not, but multiply malice in patience.
Honour is only form, form tyrant's ways.
Accuse his friends, speak doubtful, charge and praise.
Put truth to silence. People dare not see
The pride of power in formal tyranny.
I know my time, the bashas how they bend.
Faction still wakes, and competence hath spite.
'Tis fault enough that Achmat is his friend,
His lightness and his power well understood.   120
Things may so pass as Mustapha may die
Ere counsel or remorse put fury by.
But if extremity chance to require
A more audacious figure, then use rage:
It gives sometimes an honour to desire.
It shows a plainness credible to age:
While it is ruled, it may have time and place,

But if it rule, it prophesieth disgrace.
Rossa. I feel my heart now rise, my spirits work.
  Confusèd thoughts all words have overgrown.   130
  When Mustapha is dead, what star hath motion
  But Achmat, in whom Soliman yet trusts?
  They who their ends by change strive to advance
  Must never doubt to go the way of chance.
Rosten. Achmat is wise and Soliman's beloved.
  Even tyrants covet to uphold their fame,
  Not fearing evil deeds, but evil name.
Rossa. When children's blood the father's forehead stains
  What privilege for counsellors remains?
Rosten. What arguments against him?   140
Rossa.   Use of killing,
  Suspicion, the favourite of tyrants,
  Delight of change, favours past, and fear of greatness,
  Sharpened by Achmat's harsh and open dealing
  Which mighty tyrants' liberty would draw
  Into the narrow scope of human law.
Rosten. Let Mustapha be dead.
Rossa.   How dead while Achmat reigns?
  Down is the idol, but the workman lives.
  His favour, virtue, reputation, course,
  To us are still that Mustapha, or worse.   150
  Then down he must and shall. My chiefest end
  Is, first, to fix this world on my succession;
  Next, so to alter, plant, remove, create,
  That I, not he, may fashion this estate.

SCENE II

Beglerby, Rossa, Rosten

Beglerby. Rossa and Rosten! while you stand debating
  The joys or sorrows of your private fortunes,
  Some evil angel doth traduce you both.
  Achmat is called for. Wit, art, spite he hath,
  And while for sons with fathers men entreat
  Affection makes each good appearance great.

Rossa. Rosten, make haste. Go hence and carry with thee
   My life, fame, malice, fortune, and desire,
   For which, set all established things on fire.
   You ugly angels of th'infernal kingdoms,   10
   You who most bravely have maintained your beings
   In equal power, like rivals, to the heavens!
   Let me reign, while I live, in my desires,
   Or dead, live with you in eternal fires.
Beglerby. Rossa, not words, but deeds, please hell or heaven.
   I fear to tell, I tremble to conceal.
   Fortune unto the death is then displeased
   When remedies do ruin the diseased.
Rossa. Use not these parables of coward fear.
   Fear hurts less when it strikes than when it threatens.   20
Beglerby. If Mustapha shall die, his death miscarries
   Part of thy end, thy fame, thy friends, thy joy.
   Who will, to hurt his foes, himself destroy?
Rossa. Myself? what is it else but my desire?
   My brother, father, mother, and my God,
   Are but those steps which help me to aspire.
   Mustapha had never truer friend than I
   That would not with him live, but with him die.
   Yet tell: what is the worst?
Beglerby. Camena must, with him, a traitor be,   30
   Or Mustapha, for her sake, must be free.
Rossa. O cruel fates, that do in love plant woe,
   And in delights make our disasters grow.
   But speak: what hath she done?
Beglerby.   Undone thy doing,
   Discovered unto Mustapha his danger,
   And from these relics, I do more than doubt,
   Her confidence brings Soliman about.
Rossa. Now black Avernus! so I do adore thee
   As I lament my womb hath been so barren   40
   To yield but one to offer up before thee.
   Who thinks the daughters' death can mothers stay
   From ends whereon a woman's heart is fixed
   Weighs harmless nature, without passion mixed.
Beglerby. Is mother by the woman overthrown?

Rossa. Rage knows no kin: power is above the law
 And must not curious be of base respect,
 Which only they command that do neglect.
Beglerby. Your child's death angers him whom you must please.
Rossa. My ends are great. Small things are wrought with ease. 50
Beglerby. This plants confusion in the powers above.
Rossa. My end is not to quiet, but to move.
Beglerby. God plagues injustice in so great excess.
Rossa. The doing minds feel not that idleness.
Beglerby. What if this work prove not conspiracy,
 But care, that with all duties may agree?
Rossa. 'Tis private fortune that is built on truth:
 Justice is but of great estates the youth.
Beglerby. Yet by the love of mothers to their children,
 By all the pains of travail, so well known,   60
 Punish, but yet spare life: it is your own.
Rossa. I do protest no terrors, no desires,
 Glories of fame, nor rumour's injuries,
 Could, in a mother's heart, have quenched the fire
 Of loving kindness, to her children borne.
 It conquered is with nothing but with scorn.
 I am resolved to move the wheels of fate.
 Her triumph shall be pain, her glory shame.
 Horror is of excess a just reward,
 The givers of example have regard.   70

Chorus Tertius of Time: Eternity

Time

What mean these mortal children of mine own,
Ungratefully, against me to complain,
That all I build is by me overthrown?
Vices put under to rise up again?
That on my wheels both good and ill do move,
The one beneath, while th'other is above?

Day, night, hours, arts, all God or men create,
The world doth charge me that I restless change,

Suffer no being in a constant state.
Alas! why are my revolutions strange
Unto these natures made to fall or climb
With that sweet genius, ever-moving time?

What weariness, what loathsome desolations
Would plague these life- and death-begetting creatures,
Nay, what absurdity in my creations
Were it, if time-born had eternal features?
This nether orb, which is corruption's sphere,
Not being able long one shape to bear.

Could pleasure live? could worth have reverence?
Laws, arts, or sects (mere probabilities)   20
Keep up their reputation in man's sense,
If novelty did not renew his eyes,
Or time take mildly from him what he knew,
Making both me and mine to each still new?

Daughter of heaven am I; but God, none greater;
Pure like my parents; life and death of action;
Author of ill success to every creature
Whose pride against my periods makes a faction.
With me who go along, rise while they be.
Nothing of mine respects eternity.   30

Kings, why do you then blame me, whom I choose
As my anointed from the potter's ore,
And to advance you made the people lose
While you to me acknowledgèd your power?
Be confident all thrones subsist in me:
I am the measure of felicity.

Mahomet in vain, one trophy of my might,
Raised by my changed aspect to other nations,
Strives to make his succession infinite
And rob my wheels of growth, state, declination.   40
But he, and all else that would master time,
In mortal spheres shall find my power sublime.

I bring the truth to light, detect the ill.
My native greatness scorneth bounded ways.
Untimely power a few days ruin will,
Yea, worth itself falls till I list to raise.
The earth is mine; of earthly things the care
I leave to men, that, like them, earthly are.

Ripe I yet am not to destroy succession.
The vice of other kingdoms give him time.   50
The fates without me can make no progression,
By me alone, even truth doth fall or climb.
The instant petty webs, without me spun,
Untimely ended be, as they begun.

Not kings, but I, can Nemesis send forth,
The judgements of revenge and wrong are mine.
My stamps alone do warrant real worth,
How do untimely virtues else decline?
For son or father to destroy each other
Are bastard deeds, where time is not the mother.   60

Such is the work this state hath undertaken
And keeps in clouds, with purpose to advance
False counsels, in their self-craft justly shaken,
As grounded on my slave and shadow, chance.
Nay more: my child, occasion, is not free
To bring forth good or evil without me.

And shall I for revealing this misdeed,
By tying future to the present ill
Which keeps disorder's ways from happy speed,
Be guilty made of man's still-erring will?   70
Shall I, that in myself still golden am,
By their gross metal bear an iron name?

No; let man draw, by his own cursèd square,
Such crooked lines as his frail thoughts affect;
And, like things that of nothing framèd are,
Decline unto that centre of defect:

I will disclaim his downfall, and stand free,
As native rival to eternity.

Eternity

What means this new-born child of planets' motion?
This finite elf of man's vain acts and errors?   80
Whose changing wheels in all thoughts stir commotion
And in her own face only bears the mirror,
A mirror in which, since time took her fall,
Mankind sees ill increase, no good at all.

Because in your vast mouth you hold your tail,
As coupling ages past with times to come,
Do you presume your trophies shall not fail,
As both creation's cradle and her tomb?
Or, for beyond yourself you cannot see,
By days and hours would you eternal be?   90

Time is the weakest work of my creation,
And if not still repaired must straight decay.
The mortal take not my true constellation,
And so are dazzled by her nimble sway
To think her course long, which if measured right
Is but a minute of my infinite.

A minute which doth her subsistence tie,
Subsistencies which, in not being, be:
'Shall' is to come, and 'was' is passed by,
Time present cements this duplicity;   100
And if one must, of force, be like the other,
Of nothing is not nothing made the mother?

Why strives time then to parallel with me?
What be her types of longest lasting glory?
Arts, mitres, laws, moments, supremacy,
Of nature's erring alchemy the story:
From nothing sprang this point and must, by course,
To that confusion turn again, or worse.

For she, and all her mortal off-springs, build
Upon the moving base of self-conceit,   110
Which constant form can neither take nor yield,
But still change shapes, to multiply deceit:
Like playing atomi, in vain contending
Though they beginning had, to have no ending.

I that at once see time's distinct progression,
I in whose bosom 'was' and 'shall' still be,
I that in causes work th'effects' succession,
Giving both good and ill their destiny,
Though I bind all, yet can receive no bound,
But see the finite still itself confound.   120

Time, therefore know thy limits, and strive not
To make thyself or thy works infinite,
Whose essence only is to write and blot.
Thy changes prove thou hast no 'stablished right.
Govern thy mortal sphere, deal not with mine:
Time but the servant is of power divine.

Blame thou this present state, that will blame thee;
Brick-wall your errors from one to another:
Both fail alike unto eternity;
Goodness of no mixed course can be the mother.   130
Both you and yours do covet states eternal,
Whence, though pride end, your pains yet be infernal.

Ruin this mass; work change in all estates
Which, when they serve not me, are in your power:
Give unto their corruption dooms of fate;
Let your vast womb your Cadmus-men devour.
The vice yields scope enough for you and hell
To compass ill ends by not doing well.

Let Mustapha by your course be destroyed,
Let your wheels, made to wind up and untwine,   140
Leave nothing constantly to be enjoyed,
For your scythe mortal must to harm incline,

Which as this world, your maker, doth grow old,
Dooms her, for your toys, to be bought and sold.

Cross your own steps, hasten to make and mar;
With your vicissitudes please, displease your own.
Your three light wheels of sundry fashions are,
And each, by other's motion, overthrown.
Do what you can. Mine shall subsist by me.
I am the measure of felicity.   150

ACT IV, SCENE I

Soliman, Achmat

Soliman. Achmat, go, charge the bashas to assemble:
    God only is above me and consulted.
    Take freedom, not, as oft kings' servants do,
    To bind church, state, and all power under you.
    Visions are these, or bodies which appeared?
    Raised from within, or from above descending?
    Did vows lift up my soul, or bring down these?
    God's not pleased with us till our hearts find ease.
    What horror's this? *Safety, right and a crown,*
    Thrones must neglect that will adore God's light.   10
    His will, our good. Suppose it pluck us down?
    Revenge is his. Against the ill, what right?
    What means that glass borne on those glorious wings,
    Whose piercing shadows on myself reflect
    Stains which my vows against my children bring?
    My wrongs and doubts seem there despairs of vice,
    My power a turret, built against my Maker,
    My danger but disorder's prejudice.
    This glass, true mirror of the infinite,
    Shows all; yet can I nothing comprehend.   20
    This empire, nay the world, seems shadows there,
    Which mysteries dissolve me into fear.
    I that without feel no superior power,
    And feel within but what I will conceive,
    Distract, know neither what to take nor leave.

I that was free before, am now captived.
This sacrifice hath raised me from my earth,
By that I should, from that I am deprived,
In my affections man, in knowledge more,
Protected nowhere, far more disunited,   30
Still king of men but of myself no more.
In my son's death it shows this empire's fall,
And in his life my danger still included,
To die or kill, alike unnatural.
My powers and spirits with prayer thus confused,
Nor judge, nor rest, nor yield, nor reign I can,
No God, no devil, no constant king, nor man.
The earth draws one way and the sky another.
If God work thus, kings must look upwards still
And from these powers they know not choose a will.   40
Or else believe themselves, their strength, occasion,
Make wisdom conscience, and the world their sky.
So have all tyrants done; and so must I.

SCENE II

Beglerby, Soliman

Beglerby. Soliman! if Rossa you will see alive,
   You must make haste; for her despair is such
   As she thinks all things but her rage, too much.
Soliman. Fortune! hast thou not moulds enough of sorrow
   But thou must those of love and kindness borrow?
   Tell me, out of what ground grows Rossa's passion?
Beglerby. When hither I from Mustapha returned
   And had made you accompt of my commission,
   Rossa, whose heart in care for your health burned,
   Curiously after Mustapha enquiring,   10
   A token spies, which I from hence did bear,
   For Mustapha by sweet Camena wrought,
   Yet gave it not; for I began to fear,
   And something in it more than kindness thought.
   No sooner she espied this precious gift
   But, as enraged, hands on herself she lays;

From me, as one that from her self would shift,
She runs, nor till she found Camena, stays.
I follow and find both their voices high,
The one as doing, th'other suffering pain.   20
But whether your Camena live or die,
Or dead, if she by rage or guilt be slain,
If she made Rossa mad, or Rossa, mad,
To hurt things dearest to herself be glad,
I know not. But O Soliman, make haste;
For man's despair is but occasion past.

SCENE III

Rossa, Soliman, Beglerby

Rossa. What! Am I not mine own? Who dare usurp
  To take this kingdom of myself from me?
  Nature hath lied. She saith, *Life unto many*
  May be denied, but not death unto any.
  O Soliman! I have at once transgressed
  The laws of nature and thy laws of state.
  I wretched am, and you unfortunate.
Soliman. Declare what storm is this, what accident?
  Thy self-accusing doth excuse intent.
Rossa. Sir, odious is the fact on every side: 10
  The remedy is more than you can bear,
  And more must fall upon you than you fear.
Soliman. What threat'ning's this? what horror? what despite?
  Kings' thoughts to jealousy are over-tender.
Rossa. And any weakness many doth engender.
Soliman. Rossa! what means this venom of thy breath?
Rossa. Revenge and justice both require my death.
Soliman. Then tell.
Rossa.   And lose the privilege of death.
Soliman.   Then tell, and die.
Rossa. Nay, tell and live a worthy death.
  Rip not my wounds, dear lord! Silence is fit.   20
  My life hath shame, and death must cover it.
Soliman. What should be secret unto thoughts that love?

Rossa. All imperfections that offence do move.
Soliman. What guiltiness cannot goodwill forgive?
Rossa. These horrors which in stainèd souls do live.
Soliman. Are thy faults to thyself, or unto me?
Rossa. To both alike. Remediless they be.
Soliman. Yet show me trust: it proves your heart is pure
   To me, and all crimes else kings can endure.
Rossa. Imagine all the depths of wickedness,   30
   My womb as hell, my soul the world of sin,
   Confusion in my thoughts, fear merciless,
   Without me shame, impenitence within.
Soliman. These words are not of charge but intercession,
   As arguing not your guilt, but your oppression.
   Yet lest I fail, and error multiply,
   Declare what's done, what moves this agony?
Rossa. Thy child is slain. These hands embruèd are
   Even in her bowels whom I nursed with care.
Soliman. So strange a death includes some odious crime.   40
Rossa. She did conspire. Silence devours the rest.
Soliman. Horror I apprehend, danger, despair:
   All these lie hidden in this word 'Conspire'.
Rossa. This wretch conspired the ruin of this state.
   Sir! ask no more, for ills go in a blood.
   You hear already more than doth you good.
Soliman. But tell, what made Camena think this thought?
   Or by whom could she think to have it wrought?
Rossa. Mischief itself is cause of mischief done.
   What should she fear, since with her is combined   50
   Mustapha, this state's successor, and your son?
Soliman. Can this be true? is human nature such
   As in the worst part none can think too much?
Rossa. The ruins of my own may show my faith,
   For I can see no comforts after you;
   Yet to your bashas know I not what's true.
Soliman. Discover how these treasons came to light.
Rossa. Call Achmat first: for truth is but a blast
   Till it his censure's oracle hath past.
Soliman. What scorns be these? how am I thus possessed?   60
   Hath Achmat other greatness than by me?

Rossa. If greater by you than yourself he be.
Soliman. In kings the secrets of creation rest.
Rossa. Sir, you created him: he all the rest.
Soliman. I gave that to his worth, faith, industry.
Rossa. And so these gifts tied to your children be.
Soliman. What can his age expect by innovation?
Rossa. Ambition gets by doing, estimation.
Soliman. His power hath no true basis, but my grace.
Rossa. Sir, strength, like number, multiplies by place.   70
Soliman. Decrepit slave, vile creature of mine,
   Lies it in his base thoughts and shaking hands
   To move the props whereon my empire stands?
Rossa. The name of power is yours, the being, his;
   By whom creation, hope, reward and fear
   Spread, and disposèd still are, everywhere.
   Besides, there is no age in man's desire,
   Which still is active, young, and cannot rest:
   For Achmat knows you will not what you can,
   Since crowns do change a state, but not the man.   80
Soliman. His life and fortune stand upon my breath.
Rossa. Contempt deposeth kings, as well as death.
Soliman. But tell, how doth their treachery appear?
   Hath she confessed? or who doth them accuse?
Rossa. This guidon, with her own hand wrought and sent,
   Bears perfect record what was their intent.
Soliman. Expound. What is the meaning of this work
   Under whose art the arts of mischief lurk?
Rossa. These clouds, they be the house of jealousy,
   Which fire and water, both, within them bear,   90
   Where good shows less, ills greater than they be.
   Saturn here feeds on children that be his.
   His word:
   A fatal winding sheet succession is.
   This precious hill, where daintiness seems waste
   By nature's art, that all art will exceed,
   In careless fineness shows the sweet estate
   Of strength and providence together placed:
   Two intercessors reconciling hate
   And giving fear even of itself a taste.   100

Those waves, which beat upon the cliffs, do show
The cruel storms which envy hath below.
The border round about in characts hath
The mind of all, which in effect is this:
'Tis hard to know; as hard and harder too,
When men do know, to bring their hearts to do.
Soliman. What said she when you showèd her this work?
Rossa. Like them that are descried, and fain would lurk.
For while she would have made herself seem clear
She made her fault still more and more appear.   110
Soliman. How brooked she that the wicked only fear,
Her death (I mean) with what heart did she bear?
Rossa. She neither stubborn was nor overthrown,
And, but for Mustapha, made no request,
As if his harms had only been her own.
Soliman, take heed.
Malice, like clocks wound up to watch the sun,
Hasting a headlong course on many wheels,
Have never done, until they be undone.
I slew my child, my child would have slain thee: 120
All bloody fates in my blood written be.
Soliman. I swear by Mahomet, my son shall die.
Revenge is justice, and no cruelty.
Beglerby! attend. This glorious Phaeton here,
That would at once subvert this state, and me,
Safe to the eunuchs carried let him be.
These spirits of practice, that contend with fate,
Must, by their deaths, do honour to a state.

SCENE IV

Beglerby, Priest (Heli), Mustapha

Beglerby. Ah, humorous kings, how are you tossed, like waves,
With breaths that from the earth beneath you move;
Observed and betrayed, known and undone,
By being nothing, unto all things won.
Frail man! that mould'st misfortune in thy wit,
By giving thy made idol leave to fashion

Thy ends to his. For mark; what comes of it?
Nature is lost, our being only chance,
Where grace alone, not merit, must advance.
The one my image, Soliman's the other.   10
He, with himself, is wrought to spoil his own:
I, with myself, am made the instrument
That courts should have no great hearts innocent.
But stay! why wander I thus from my ends?
New counsels must be had when planets fall:
Change hath her periods, and is natural.
The saint we worship is authority,
Which lives in kings, and cannot with them die.
True faith makes martyrs unto God alone:
Misfortune hath no such odds in a throne.   20
But see! This foot-ball to the stars is come,
Mustapha I mean, in innocence secure,
Which, for it will not give fate, must endure.
Heli distract, fixed and aghast I see,
And will go nearer to observe the rest,
That wit may take occasion at the best.
For if they feel their state and know their strength,
How prone this mass is for another head,
Did ever hazard find occasion dead?
Whether he get the crown or lose his blood,   30
The one is ill to him: to me both good.
Priest. False Mahomet! Thy laws monarchal are,
Unjust, ambitious, full of spoil and blood,
Having not of the best, but greatest, care.
Must life yield up itself to be put out,
Before this frame of nature be decayed?
Must blood the tribute be of tyrants' doubt?
O wretched flesh! in which must be obeyed
God's law, that wills impossibility,
And princes' wills, the gulfs of tyranny.   40
We priests, even with the mystery of words,
First bind ourselves, and with ourselves the rest
To servitude, the sheath of tyrant's sword,
Each worst unto himself approving best.
    People! believe in God: we are untrue,

And spiritual forges under tyrants' might:
God only doth command what's good for you,
Where we do preach your bodies to the war,
Your goods to tax, your freedom unto bands,
Duties by which you owned of others are   50
And fear, which to your harms doth lend your hands.
Ah, forlorn wretch! with my hypocrisy,
I Mustapha have ruined, and this state.
I am the evil's friend, hell's mediator,
A fury unto man, a man to furies.

Mustapha. Whence grows this sudden rage thy gesture utters?
These agonies, and furious blasphemings?
Man then doth show his reason is defaced
When rage thus shows itself with reason graced.

Priest. If thou have felt the self-accusing war   60
Where knowledge is the endless hell of thought,
The ruins of my soul there figured are,
For where despair the conscience doth fear
My wounds bleed out that horror which they bear.

Mustapha. Horror and pride, in nature opposite,
The one makes error great, the other small:
Where rooted habits have no sense at all.
Heli, judge not thyself with troubled mind,
But show thy heart: when passion's steams breathe forth
Even woes we wondered at are nothing worth.   70

Priest. I have offended nature, God, and thee:
To each a sin, to all impiety.

Mustapha. The faults of man are finite, like his merits:
His mercies infinite that judgeth spirits.
Tell me thy errors, teach me to forgive,
Which he that cannot do knows not to live.

Priest. Canst thou forgive? Rather avoid the cause
Which else makes mercy more severe than laws.

Mustapha. From man to man duties are but respects,
The grounds whereof are mere humanity:
Can justice other there than mercy be?   80

Priest. Thought is an act. Who can forgive remorse,
Where nature, by her own law, suffers force?

Mustapha. What shall I do? Tell me. I do not fear.

Priest. Preserve thy father, with thyself, and me:
  Else guilty of each other's death we be.
Mustapha. Tell how.
Priest.   Thy father purposeth thy death.
  I did advise: thou offerest up thy breath.
Mustapha. What have I to my father done amiss?
Priest. That wicked Rossa thy stepmother is.   90
Mustapha. Wherein have I of Rossa ill deserved?
Priest. In that the empire is for thee reserved.
Mustapha. Is it a fault to be my father's son?
  Ah, foul ambition, which, like water-floods
  Not channel-bound, dost neighbours over-run,
  And growest nothing when thy rage is done.
  Must Rossa's heirs out of my ashes rise?
  Yet Zanger, I acquit thee of my blood,
  For, I believe, thy heart hath no impression
  To ruin Mustapha for his succession.   100
  But tell what colours they against me use,
  And how my father's love they first did wound.
Priest. Of treason towards him they thee accuse:
  Thy fame and greatness gives their malice ground.
Mustapha. Good world, where it is danger to be good!
  Yet grudge I not power of myself to Power.
  This baseness only in mankind I blame,
  That indignation should give laws to fame.
  Show me the truth. To what rules am I bound?
Priest. No man commanded is by God to die,   110
  As long as he may persecution fly.
Mustapha. To fly hath scorn. It argues guiltiness,
  Inherits fear, weakly abandons friends,
  Gives tyrants fame, takes honour from distress.
  Death! do thy worst. Thy greatest pains have end.
Priest. Mischief is like the cockatrice's eyes,
  Sees first, and kills; or is seen first, and dies.
  Fly to thy strength, which makes misfortune vain.
  Rossa intends thy ruin. What is she?
  Seek in her bowels for thy father lost.   120
  Who can redeem a king with viler cost?
Mustapha. O false and wicked colours of desire!

Anarchy is called for here by discontent.
To Mustapha I know the world's affection.
To Soliman fear only draws regard,
And men stir easily where the rein is hard.
Then let them stir, and tear away this veil
Of pride from power; that our great lord may see
Unmiracled, his own humanity.
People! look up above this Divan's name,
This vent of error, snare of liberty,
Where punishment is tyrant's tax and fame.   210
Abolish these false oracles of might,
Courts subaltern, which, bearing tyrant's seal,
Oppress the people and make vain appeal.
Ruin these specious masks of tyranny,
These crown-paid Cadis of their maker's fashion:
Which, power-like, for right distribute passion,
Confound degrees, the artifice of thrones
To bear down nature while they raise up art
With gilded titles to deceive the heart.
The church absolves you, truth approves your work.   220
Craft and oppression everywhere God hates.
Besides, where order is not, change is free,
And gives all rights to popularity.

Chorus Quartus of converts to Mahomedanism

Angels fell first from God, man was the next that fell:
Both being made by Him for heaven, have for themselves made
    hell.
Defection had, for ground, an essence which might fall,
Grown proud with glories of that God, like whom they would
    be all.
Hence each thing but himself these fall'n powers comprehend,
Nor can beyond deprivings ill their knowledges extend.
But in that darkened orb, through mists which vice creates,
Joyless, enjoy a woeful glimpse of their once happy states;
And serpent-like, with cursed eternity of evil,
Active in mischief many ways to add more to the devil,   10
They take on every shape of vice that may delight,

Striving to make creation less, privation infinite.
Whence man from goodness strayed, and wisdom's innocence,
Yea subject made to grave and hell, by error's impotence,
Labours, with shadowed light of imbecility,
To raise more towers of Babel up, above the truth to be.
Among which phantasms mounts that roof of tyrant's power,
The outward Church, whose nature is her founders to devour.
And through an hollow charm of life-forsaken words,
Entangle real things, to reign on all the earth affords: 20
By irreligious rites helping religion's name
To blemish truth, with gilded lies cast in opinion's frame.
Whence she that erst raised kings by pulling freedom down
Now seeks to free inferior powers, and only bind the Crown.
In which aspiring pride, where wit encount'reth wit,
The power of thrones unequal is and turns the scale with it,
Mast'ring those greedy swarms of superstitious rites
Which by the sinner's fear, not faith, makes her scope infinite.
Hence grows it that our priests, erst oracles of state,
Against whose doom our sultans durst trust nothing unto   30
        fate,
At once were censured all, in one house to the fire,
As guilty in their idle souls of Icarus' desire.
So free, and easy is it to cast down again
The creature's pride, which his creator covets to restrain:
Again, so easy is it to bring states to death
By urging those powers to oppose, whose union gave them
        breath.
Thus from the lives of priests kings first their doctrine stain
And then let sect, schism, question in, to qualify their reign.
Nor can this swoll'n excess be well reformed in either
While both stand mixed of good and ill which join not well   40
        together.
Kings seeking from the Church the rites of deity,
The Church from kings, not nursing help, but God's
        supremacy.
A strife wherein they both find loss instead of gain,
Since neither state can stand alone, much less divided reign.
The strife and peace of which (like ocean ebbs and floods)
Successively do here contract and there disperse our goods.

And by this mutual spleen amongst these sovereign parts
While each seeks gain by other's loss, the universal smarts.
For as souls, made to reign, when they let down their state
Into the body's humours, straight those humours give them   50
    fate,
So, when the Church and Crown (the souls of empire) fall
Into contempt, which human power cannot subsist withal,
They strive, turn and descend, feel error's destiny,
Which in a well-formed empire is a vagabond to be.
Thus, in disorder's chain, while each link wresteth other,
Incestous Error to her own is made both child and mother.
So as their doing is undoings still to breed,
And fatally entomb again each other in each deed.
Hence human laws appealed, as moderators come,
Who, under show of compromise, take on them sovereign   60
    doom,
Ent'ring in at the first, like wisdom, with applause,
And though propounded from our faults, yet, by consent, made
    laws,
Or rather scales, to weigh opinion with the truth
Which, like stepmothers, often bring the better side to ruth.
And as of active ill (from whence they took their root)
Guilty, and so not strong to stand upon a constant foot,
They wave, strive, and aspire, can bear no weight above,
But, as with sovereign power itself and nothing else in love,
That rival spleen, which equals still to equals bear,
Forgotten, or asleep, as if desire had conquered fear,   70
They factiously a peace with their chief rival make,
And let in wars, which like a flood, all sea-banks over-rake.
In which one act laws prove, though nature gave them ground,
That they both mould and practice took from war, which hath
    no bound.
Because, like Mars his seed, they feed upon their own,
And by the spoil of crowns and men take glory to be known.
In which dear interchange between church, laws and might,
While all their counsels are allayed by overacting right,
They leave their supreme pitch to servile craft impawned,
Descending each to traffic there, where he ought to   80
    command.

Till fondly thus engaged into a civil war,
They casting off all public ends do only make to mar.
Yet keep a scope in show to counterpoise each other,
And save the health and honour up of Monarchy their
    mother.
But as in man, whose frame is chiefly four complexions,
Really joined, dispersèd, mixed with opposite connections,
When any of these four fold or distract too far,
Diseases reign, which but disorder's native children are;
From which contention stirred 'twixt nature and her foes,
While humour weaken humour doth, to health the body   90
    grows:
So in these divers powers, excess of opposition
Oft, by begetting strange diseases, proves the state's physician.
Mavors, that monster, born of many-headed passion,
While it seems to destroy all moulds, to each mould giving
    fashion.
Yet as these elements, thus opposite in kind,
While balanced by superior ties they live as if combined,
To make their discords base unto that harmony
In whose sweet union mildly linked all powers concur to be;
When any breaks too much that poise wherein they stood,
To make his own subsistence firm, with show of common   100
    good;
By overacting, straight it breaks that well-built frame,
Wherein their being stood entire, although they lost their name:
So in that noble work of public government
When Crowns, Church, soldiers, or the laws, do overmuch
    dissent,
That frame wherein they lived, is fatally dissolved,
And each in gulfs of self-conceit, as fatally, involved.
Thus reels our present state, and her foundation waves,
By making trophies of times past, of present time the graves.
Laws strive to curb the Church, the Church wounds laws
    again;
The soldier would have Church, Throne, laws kept low   110
    that he might reign.
And as before, while they joined to make empire large,
All unto greatness raisèd were, by doing well their charge,

So now, by pulling quills each from the other's wings,
They jointly all are cried down, by letting fall their kings.
A fate prepared to shake that Ottoman succession,
Which erst, removèd from men's eyes, wrought reverend
   impression.
Where now this sultan's line prophaned when men shall see,
They soon will scorn grace, hope and fear, the sceptre's
   mystery.
Nor will they more by faith or zeal in war be led
To sacrifice their lives to power, for fame when they be   120
   dead.
Or, to shun mortal pains, provoke the infinite:
Wrong in man's nature stirring sparks that give both heat and
   light
To gather in again those strengths they gave away,
And so pluck down that Samson's post, on which our sultans stay.

ACT V, SCENE I

Zanger, solus

Nourished in court, where no thought's peace is nourished,
Used to behold the tragedies of ruin,
Brought up with fears that follow princes' fortunes,
Yet am I like him that hath lost his knowledge,
Or never heard one story of misfortune.
My heart doth fall away: fear falls upon me.
Tame rumours that have been mine old acquaintance
Are to me now (like monsters) fear, or wonder.
My love begins to plague me with suspicions.
My mother's promises of my advancement,   10
The name of Mustapha so often murmured,
With whose name ever I have been rejoicèd,
Now makes my heart misgive, my spirits languish.
Man then is augur of his own misfortune,
When his joy yields him arguments of anguish.

ACT V, SCENE II

Achmat, Zanger

Achmat. Tyrants! Why swell you thus against your makers?
   Is raised equality so soon grown wild?
   Dare you deprive your people of succession
   Which thrones and sceptres on their freedoms build?
   Have fear or love in greatness no impression?
   Since people who did raise you to the crown,
   Are ladders standing still to let you down.
Zanger. Achmat! What strange events beget these passions?
Achmat. Nature is ruined, humanity fall'n asunder,
   Our Alcoran prophaned, empire defaced,   10
   Ruin is broken loose, truth dead, hope banished.
   My heart is full, my voice and spirits tremble.
Zanger. Yet tell the worst.
   By counsel or comparison things lessen.
Achmat. No counsel or comparison can lessen
   The loss of Mustapha, so vilely murdered,
Zanger. How? dead? what chance or malice hath prevented
   Mankind's good fortune?
Achmat.   Father's unkindly doubts.
Zanger. Tell how.
Achmat.   When Soliman, by cunning spite
   Of Rossa's witchcrafts, from his heart had banished   20
   Justice of kings and lovingness of fathers,
   To wage and lodge such camps of heady passions
   As that sect's cunning practices could gather,
   Envy took hold of worth, doubt did misconster,
   Renown was made a lie, and yet a terror:
   Nothing could calm his rage or move compassion:
   Mustapha must die. To which end fetched he was,
   Laden with hopes and promises of favour.
   So vile a thing is craft in every heart
   As it makes Power itself descend to art.   30
   While Mustapha, that neither hoped nor feared,
   Seeing the storms of rage and danger coming,
   Yet came, and came accompanied with power.

But neither power, which warranted his safety,
Nor safety that makes violence a justice,
Could hold him from obedience to this throne:
A gulf which hath devourèd many a one.
Zanger. Alas! Could neither truth appease his fury,
Nor his unlooked humility of coming,
Nor any secret witnessing remorses?
Can nature from herself make such divorces?   40
Tell on, that all the world may rue and wonder.
Achmat. There is a place environèd with trees,
Upon whose shadowed centre there is pitched
A large embroidered, sumptuous pavilion,
The stately throne of tyranny and murder,
Where mighty men are slain before they know
That they to other than to honour go.
Mustapha no sooner to the port did come,
But thither he is sent for and conducted
By six slave eunuchs, either taught to colour   50
Mischief with reverence or forced, by nature,
To reverence true virtue in misfortune.
While Mustapha, whose heart was now resolvèd,
Not fearing death, which he might have prevented,
Nor craving life, which he might well have gotten
If he would other duties have forgotten,
Yet glad to speak his last thoughts to his father,
Desired the eunuchs to entreat it for him.
They did; wept they; and kneelèd to his father.   60
But bloody rage, that glories to be cruel,
And jealousy that fears she is not fearful,
Made Soliman refuse to hear or pity.
He bids them haste their charge, and, bloody-eyed,
Beholds his son whilst he, obeying, died.
Zanger. How did that doing heart endure to suffer?
Tell on.
Quicken my powers hardened and dull to good,
Which yet unmoved hear tell of brother's blood.
Achmat. While these six eunuchs to this charge appointed   70
(Whose hearts had never used their hands to pity,
Whose hands, now only, trembled to do murder)

With reverence and fear, stood still, amazèd,
Loth to cut off such worth, afraid to save it:
Mustapha with thoughts resolvèd, and united,
Bids them fulfil their charge and look no further.
Their hearts afraid to let their hands be doing,
The cord, that hateful instrument of murder,
They lifting up, let fall, and falling, lift it.
Each sought to help, and helping, hindered other.   80
Till Mustapha, in haste to be an angel,
With heavenly smiles and quiet words foreshows
The joy and peace of those souls where he goes.
His last words were: 'O father! now forgive me;
Forgive them too that wrought my overthrow.
Let my grave never minister offences.
For since my father coveteth my death,
Behold, with joy, I offer him my breath.'
　　The eunuchs roar. Soliman his rage is glutted.
His thoughts divine of vengeance for this murder.   90
Rumour flies up and down. The people murmur.
Sorrow gives laws before men know the truth;
Fear prophesieth aloud, and threatens ruth.
Zanger. Remiss and languished are men's coward spirits,
Where God forbids revenge and patience too.
Yet to the dead nature ordaineth rites,
Which idle love, I feel, hath power to do.
I will go hence and show to them that live
That God almighty cannot all forgive.   100

SCENE III

Rosten. Help, Achmat, help! Fury runs over all.
Pity my state that with the empire fall.
Achmat. What sound is this of ruin and confusion?
Terror afraid? cruelty come for pity?
Seditious Rosten, running from sedition?
And malice forced to enemies for succour?
Rosten. Achmat! the mysteries of empire are dissolved.
Fury hath made the people know their forces.
Majesty (as but a mist), they breed and spread.

Nothing but things impossible will please.   10
Mustapha must live again, or Rosten perish.
Oh wretchedness! which I cannot deny;
I am ashamed to live and loth to die.
Achmat. Tell on the dangers which concern the state.
For thee, thou rod ordained unto the fire,
Thy other dooms let Acheron enquire.
Rosten. When Mustapha was by the eunuchs strangled,
Forthwith his camp grew doubtful of his absence,
The guard of Soliman himself did murmur.
People began to search their prince's counsels.   20
Fury gave laws, the laws of duty vanished,
kind fear of him they loved self-fear had banished.
The headlong spirits were the heads that guided;
He that most disobeyed was most obeyed.
Fury so suddenly became united,
As while her forces nourishèd confusion,
Confusion seemed with discipline delighted.
Towards Soliman they run: and as the waters
That meet with banks of snow, make snow grow water,
So even those guards that stood to interrupt them   30
Give easy passage and pass on amongst them.
    Soliman, who saw this storm of mischief coming,
Thinks absence his best argument unto them:
Retires himself and sends me to demand
What they demanded, or what meant their coming?
I spake: they cried, 'For Mustapha and Achmat.'
Some bid 'away'; some 'kill'; some 'save'; some 'hearken'.
Those that cried 'save' were those that sought to kill me.
Who cried 'hark' were those that first brake silence.
They held, that bade me go. Humility was guilty,   40
Words were reproach, silence in me was scornful.
They answered ere they asked; assured, and doubted.
I fled; their fury followed to destroy me.
Fury made haste, haste multiplied their fury.
Each would do all, none would give place to other.
The hindmost strake, and while the foremost lifted
Their arms to strike, each weapon hindered other.
Their running let their strokes, strokes let their running.

Desire, mortal enemy to desire,
Made them that sought my life give life unto me.   50
Now Achmat! Though blood-thirst deserve no pity,
Malice no love, though just revenge be mercy,
Yet save me. For although my death be lawful,
The judges and the manner are unlawful.
If I die, what hath Soliman for warrant?
Mischief is still the governess of mischief.
If Soliman be slain, where will they stay
That thorough God and majesty make way?
Achmat. Rosten! Dar'st thou name duty, laws or mercy?
    Owe not thyself to him thou would'st destroy.   60
    Make good thy love of murder: die with joy.
Rosten. If Soliman, who hath been thy best fortune,
    Safe thou wilt see, or safe his state preserve,
    Make haste. The state did never ill deserve.
Achmat. Occasion! when art thou more glorious,
    Than even now, when thou requir'st of me
    To fall with states in common destiny?
    States trespass not. Tyrants they be that swerve
    And bring upon all empires age, or death,
    By making truth but only princes' breath.   70
    This monarchy first rose by industry,
    Honour held up by universal fame,
    Stirring men's minds to strange audacity.
    Great ends procured our armies greater name,
    To enemies no injury had blame;
    Worth was not proud, authority was wise,
    And did not on her own then tyrannise.

    Now owned by humour of this dotard king
    (Who, swoll'n with practice of long government,
    Doth stain the public with ill managing)   80
    Honour is laid asleep, fame is unbent:
    His will, his end; and Power's right everywhere:
    Now, what can this but dissolution bear?
    Whether our choice or nature gave us kings,
    The end of either was the good of all:
    Where many strengths make this omnipotence,
    The good of many there is natural.

One draws from all: can that be fortunate?
All leave this one: can this be injury?
    And shall I help to stay the people's rage   90
From this estate, thus ruinèd with age?
No, people, no. Question these thrones of tyrants.
Revive your old equalities of nature.
Authority is more than that she maketh.
Lend not your strengths to keep your own strengths under.
Proceed in fury. Fury hath law and reason
Where it doth plague the wickedness of treason.
For when whole kingdoms surfeit, and must fall,
Justice divides not there, but ruins all.
Besides of duties 'twixt the earth and sky   100
He can observe no one that cannot die.
But stay! shall man, the dam and grave of crowns
With mutiny pull sacred sceptres down?
People of wisdom void, with passion filled,
While they keep names, still press to ruin things.
Freedom dissolves them; order they refuse.
Worth, freedom, power and right while they destroy,
Worth, freedom, power and right they would enjoy.
What soul then, loving nature, duty, order,
Would hold a life of such a stateless state,   110
As, made of humours, must give honour fate?
    No, Achmat! Rather, with thy hazard, strive
To save this high raised sovereignity,
Under whose wings there was prosperity.
I yield. But how?
Force is impossible, for that is theirs.
Counsel shows like their enemy, delay.
Order turns all desires into fears.
Their art is violence, and chance their end.
What, but occasion, there can be my friend?   120
Behold where Rossa comes, in her looks varying
Like rage, that with itself still fears miscarrying.

SCENE IV

Rossa, Achmat

Rossa. Whoever thinks by virtue to aspire
    And goodness dreams to be but fortune's star,
    Or who by mischief's wit seeks his desire,
    And thinks no conscience ways to honour are:
    He, Mustapha! here seeing thee and me,
    Sees no man's good or ill rules destiny.
    Then ah! woe worth them that with God contend,
    And would exchange the course of fate by wit,
    Which God makes work to bring his works to end
    And with itself, even, oft doth ruin it.   10
    Ah tyrant fate! to them that do amiss,
    For nothing left me but my error is,
Achmat. What glory's this, that with itself is sad?
    Good luck makes all hearts, but the guilty, glad.
Rossa. Zanger, for whom even Mustapha was slain,
    And unto whom Camena's blood was shed,
    Zanger, for whom all worlds on me complain,
    Hath done that which nor law nor truth could do,
    (Horror and doubt in my desires breed)
    Murthered himself, and overthrown me too.   20
Achmat. Tell why, and how, he so unthankful died.
Rossa. In every creature's heart there lives desire,
    Which men do hallow as appearing good,
    For greatness they esteem it to aspire
    Although it weakness be, well understood.
    This unbound, raging, infinite thought-fire
    I took—nay it took me—and placed my heart
    On hopes to alter empire and succession.
    Chance was my faith and order my despair,
    Sect, innovation, change of princes' right   30
    My studies were. I thought hope had no end
    In her, that hath an emperor to friend.
    Whence, like the storms (that then like storms do blow,
    When all things but themselves, they overthrow),
    I ventured: first to make the father fear,

Then hate, then kill, his most beloved child.
My daughter did discover him my way.
To Mustapha she opened mine intent;
For she had tried, but could not turn my heart.
Yet no hurt to me she in telling meant,   40
Though hurt she did me to disclose my art.
I sought revenge—revenge it could not be,
For, I confess, she never wrongèd me.
Remorse that hath a faction in each heart,
Womanish shame, which is compassion's friend,
Conspired with truth to have restrainèd me,
Yet killed I her whom I did dearly love.
Furies of choice, what arguments can move?
I killed her, for I thought her death would prove
That truth, not hate, made Mustapha suspected.   50
The more it seemed against a mother's love,
The more it showed I Soliman affected:
Thus, underneath severe and upright dealing,
A mischievous stepmother's malice stealing.
It took effect, for few mean ill in vain.
Which wicked art, although the father knew,
Yet his affection turned my ill to good,
Vice but of hers, being only understood.
Fear grew discreet, and would not speak in vain,
Courage turned all the strengths of heart to bear.   60
Justice itself durst murmur, not complain.
So little care the fates for us below:
So little men fear God they do not know.
    But ah! woe worth each false preposterous way,
Which promiseth good luck to evil deeds,
Since Mustapha, whose death I made my glory
Hath left me no power now but to be sorry.
For Zanger, when he saw his brother dead,
Confusedly, with divers shapes distract,
He silent stood, with horrors compassèd,   70
His duty mixed with woe, kindness with rage,
Reverence, revenge, both representing shame,
Equally against, and with, a mother's name.
But as these shadows vanished from his mind,

The globes of his enragèd eyes he threw
On me, like nature justly made unkind,
And for this hateful fault my love did make
From pity, woe, and anger, thus he spake:
'Mother! Is this the way of woman's heart?
Have you no law or God, but will, to friend? 80
Can neither power, nor goodness 'scape your art?
Be these the counsels by which you ascend?
Is there no hell, or do the devils love fire?
If neither God, heaven, hell, or devil be,
'Tis plague enough that I am born of thee.
Mother! O monstrous name! shall it be said
That thou hast done this fact for Zanger's sake?
Honour and life, shall they to me upbraid
That from thy mischief they their honour take?
O wretched men! which under shame are laid 90
For faults which we, and which our parents, make.
Yet Rossa! to be thine in this I glory
That, being thine, gives power to make thee sorry.'
He wounds his heart, and falling down with death
On Mustapha, who there for his sake died,
These words he spake:
'Ah base ambition! mould of cruelty,
In thy vast narrow bosom ever breed
These hideous counsels, light-abhorring deeds.
Yet you pure souls that Mahomet adore, 100
Read in these wounds my horror of his death,
And to the Christians carry thou it, breath'.
He dies. Woe's me. When in my heart I look,
Horror I see, all there lost, but despair,
My love and joy become affliction's book,
Eternity of shame is printed there.
   To think of God! Alas, that so I may,
Yet power and goodness can but show me fear.
Mercy I cannot crave, that cannot trust,
Nor die I will, for death concludeth pains. 110
Nor languish in conceit, for then I must
Abhor my soul, in which all mischiefs reign.
I will bear with me in this body's dust

id) was one reason why Sir Philip did cover that glorious
enterprise with a cloud. Another was because in the doing, while
t passed unknown he knew it would pass without interruption,
and when it was done presumed the success would put envy and
all her agents to silence.

On the other side Sir Francis found that Sir Philip's friends,
with the influence of his excellent inward powers, would add
both weight and fashion to his ambition, and consequently,
either with or without Sir Philip's company, yield unexpected
ease and honour to him in this voyage.

Upon these two divers counsels they treat confidently together; the preparations go on with a large hand amongst our
governors; nothing is denied Sir Francis that both their pro-
pounding hearts could demand. To make which expedition of
less difficulty they kept the particular of this plot more secret
than it was possible for them to keep the general preparations of
so great a journey, hoping that while the Spaniard should be
forced to arm everywhere against them, he could not anywhere
be so royally provided to defend himself but they might land
without any great impediment.

In these terms Sir Francis departs for Plymouth with his ships,
vowed and resolved that when he stayed for nothing but for a
wind, the watch-word should come post for Sir Philip. The time
of the year made haste away and Sir Francis to follow it either
made more haste than needed or at least seemed to make more
50 than really he did. Notwithstanding, as I dare aver that in his
own element he was industrious, so dare I not condemn his
affections in this misprision of time. Howsoever a letter comes
post for Sir Philip as if the whole fleet stayed only for him and the
wind. In the mean-season, the state hath intelligence that Don
Antonio was at sea for England and resolved to land at Plymouth.
Sir Philip turning occasion into wisdom, puts himself into the
employment of conducting up this king, and under that veil
leaves the court without suspicion, over-shoots his father-in-law,
then Secretary of State, in his own bow; comes to Plymouth; was
60 feasted the first night by Sir Francis with a great deal of outward
pomp and compliment.

Yet I, that had the honour as of being bred with him from his
youth, so now (by his own choice of all England) to be his loving

What curse soever to the earth remains.
I will bear with me envy, rage, desire,
To set all hearts, all times, all worlds on fire.
You weak souls! whose true love hath made you base,
And fixed your quiets upon others' will:
You humble hearts! which unto power give place,
For conscience bearing yokes of tyrants' skill: 120
You poor religious! who in hope of grace
Bear many sore temptations of the ill,
Rejoice: unkindness, cruelty, disgrace,
Vengeance and wrong bear hence with me I will.
Rather take heed: Where can more danger be
Than where these powers may be disposed by me?

Chorus Quintus, Tartarorum

Vast superstition! Glorious style of weakness!
Sprung from the deep disquiet of man's passion,
To desolation and despair of nature:
Thy texts bring princes' titles into question,
Thy prophets set on work the sword of tyrants.
They manacle sweet truth with their distinctions,
Let virtue blood, teach cruelty for God's sake,
Fashioning one God, yet him of many fashions,
Like many-headed error, in their passions.

Mankind! Trust not these superstitious dreams,   10
Fear's idols, pleasure's relics, sorrow's pleasures.
They make the wilful hearts their holy temples,
The rebels unto government their martyrs.

No, thou child of false miracles begotten!
False miracles, which are but ignorance of cause,
Lift up the hopes of thy abjected prophets.
Courage and worth abjure thy painted heavens,
Sickness thy blessings are, misery thy trial,
Nothing, thy way unto eternal being,
Death to salvation, and the grave to heaven.   20
So blessed be they, so angeled, so eternised
That tie their senses to thy senseless glories,
And die, to cloy the after-age with stories.

Man should make much of life, as nature's table
Wherein she writes the cypher of her glory.
Forsake not nature, nor misunderstand her,
Her mysteries are read without faith's eye-sight.
She speaketh in our flesh, and from our senses
Delivers down her wisdoms to our reason.
If any man would break her laws to kill,   30
Nature doth, for defence, allow offences.
She neither taught the father to destroy,
Nor promised any man, by dying, joy.

Chorus Sacerdotum

Oh wearisome condition of humanity!
Born under one law, to another bound:
Vainly begot, and yet forbidden vanity,
Created sick, commanded to be sound:
What meaneth nature by these divers laws?
Passion and reason self-division cause:
Is it the mark or majesty of power
To make offences that it may forgive?
Nature herself doth her own self deflower
To hate those errors she herself doth give.   10
For how should man think that he may not do
If nature did not fail, and punish too?
Tyrant to others, to herself unjust,
Only commands things difficult and hard.
Forbids us all things, which it knows we lust,
Makes easy pains, unpossible reward.
If nature did not take delight in blood,
She would have made more easy ways to good.
We that are bound by vows, and by promotion,
With pomp of holy sacrifice and rites,   20
To teach belief in God and stir devotion,
To preach of heaven's wonders and delights:
Yet when each of us in his own heart looks,
He finds the God there far unlike his books.

LIFE OF SIR PHILIP SIDN[EY]

This work was originally designed by Greville as a dedica[-]
tion of his poems to the memory of Sidney, the friend [...]
includes a notable defence of the Earl of Essex, executed f[or]
in 1601, and also an extensive essay in praise of Queen E[...]
extracts here chosen fall into three groups: lively biograph[y]
(I and II), judgements upon great figures of his time (III, [...]
and Greville's comments on his intentions and achievement[...]
poetry (VI and VII).

I. A FRUSTRATED EXPEDITION TO THE WEST [INDIES]

The next step which he [Sidney] intended into the worl[d...]
expedition of his own projecting, wherein he fashioned th[...]
body with purpose to become head of it himself, I mean [...]
employment but one of Sir Francis Drake to the West [...]
Which journey, as the scope of it was mixed both of sea an[d...]
service, so had it accordingly distinct officers and comma[...]
chosen by Sir Philip out of the ablest governors of those m[...]
times. The project was contrived between themselves in [...]
manner, that both should equally be governors when they [...]
left the shores of England, but while things were a-preparing [...]
home, Sir Francis was to bear the name and by the credit of [...]
Philip have all particulars abundantly supplied.

The reason of which secret carriage was the impossibility f[or]
Sir Philip to win the Queen or government (out of the valu[e]
which they rated his worth at) to dispense with an employment
for him so remote and of so hazardous a nature. Besides his credit
and reputation with the state lay not that way; so as our provident magistrates, expecting a prenticeship more seriously in
martial than mechanical actions and therein measuring all men
by one rule, would (as Sir Philip thought) not easily believe his
inexperience equal for a design of so many divers and dangerous
passages: howsoever wise men, even in the most active times,
have determined this art of government to be rather a riches of
nature than any proper fruit of industry or education. This (as I

and beloved Achates in this journey, observing the countenance of this gallant mariner more exactly than Sir Philip's leisure served him to do, after we were laid in bed, acquainted him with my observation of the discountenance and depression which appeared in Sir Francis, as if our coming were both beyond his expectation and desire. Nevertheless, that ingenuous spirit of Sir Philip's, though apt to give me credit yet not apt to discredit others, made him suspend his own and labour to change or qualify my judgement; till within some few days after, finding the ships neither ready according to promise nor possibly to be made ready in many days, and withal observing some sparks of false fire breaking out unawares from his yoke-fellow daily, it pleased him, in the freedom of our friendship, to return me my own stock with interest.

All this while Don Antonio lands not; the fleet seemed to us (like the weary passenger's inn) still to go further from our desires; letters came from the court to hasten it away: it may be the leaden feet and nimble thoughts of Sir Francis wrought in the day and unwrought by night while he watched an opportunity to discover us, without being discovered.

For within a few days after, a post steals up to the court upon whose arrival an alarm is presently taken, messengers sent away to stay us, or, if we refused, to stay the whole fleet. Notwithstanding, this first Mercury, his errand being partly advertised to Sir Philip beforehand, was intercepted upon the way, his letters taken from him by two resolute soldiers in mariner's apparel, brought instantly to Sir Philip, opened and read. The contents as welcome as bulls of excommunication to the superstitious Romanist when they enjoin him either to forsake his right or his holy Mother-Church, yet did he sit this first process without noise or answer.

The next was a more imperial mandate, carefully conveyed and delivered to himself by a peer of this realm, carrying with it in the one hand grace, the other thunder. The grace was an offer of instant employment under his uncle, then going General into the Low Countries; against which, although he would gladly have demurred, yet the confluence of reason, transcendency of power, fear of staying the whole fleet, made him instantly sacrifice all these selfnesses to the duty of obedience.

I. SIDNEY'S FATAL WOUND AT ZUTPHEN

. . . I will cut off his actions as God did his life, in the midst; and so conclude with his death.

In which passage, though the pride of flesh and glory of mankind be commonly so alloyed as the beholders seldom see anything else in it but objects of horror and pity; yet had the fall of this man such natural degrees, that the wound whereof he died made rather an addition than diminution to his spirits. So that he showed the world, in a short progress to a long home, passing fair and well-drawn lines, by the guide of which all pilgrims of this life may conduct themselves humbly into the haven of everlasting rest.

When that unfortunate stand was to be made before Zutphen to stop the issuing out of the Spanish army from a straight, with what alacrity soever he went to actions of honour, yet remembering that upon just grounds the ancient sages describe the worthiest persons to be ever best armed, he had completely put on his; but meeting the marshal of the camp lightly armed (whose honour in that art would not suffer this unenvious Themistocles to sleep) the unspotted emulation of his heart, to venture without any inequality, made him cast off his cuisses; and so, by the secret influence of destiny, to disarm that part where God, it seems, had resolved to strike him. Thus they go on, every man in the head of his own troop; and, the weather being misty, fell unawares upon the enemy who had made a strong stand to receive them near to the very walls of Zutphen; by reason of which accident their troops fell not only unexpectedly to be engaged within the level of the great shot that played from the rampiers, but more fatally within shot of their muskets which were laid in ambush within their own trenches.

Now whether this were a desperate cure in our leaders for a desperate disease; or whether misprision, neglect, audacity or what else induced it, it is no part of my office to determine, but only to make the narration clear and deliver rumour, as it passed then, without any stain or enamel.

However, by this stand, an unfortunate hand out of those forespoken trenches, brake the bone of Sir Philip's thigh with a musket-shot. The horse he rode upon was rather furiously choleric than bravely proud and so forced him to forsake the field, but not his back, as the noblest and fittest bier to carry a martial commander to his grave. In which sad progress, passing along by the rest of the army where his uncle the General was and being thirsty with excess of bleeding, he called for drink, which was presently brought him; but as he was putting the bottle to his mouth, he saw a poor soldier carried along, who had eaten his last at the same feast, ghastly casting up his eyes at the bottle. Which Sir Philip perceiving, took it from his head before he drank and delivered it to the poor man with these words, 'Thy necessity is yet greater than mine.' And when he had pledged this poor soldier, he was presently carried to Arnheim.

III. AN ACCOUNT OF SIDNEY

Indeed he was a true model of worth; a man fit for conquest, plantation, reformation, or what action soever is greatest and hardest amongst men: withall, such a lover of mankind and goodness, that whosoever had any real parts in him found comfort, participation, and protection to the uttermost of his power; like Zephyrus he giving life where he blew. The universities abroad and at home accounted him a general Maecenas of learning, dedicated their books to him, and communicated every invention, or improvement of knowledge with him. Soldiers honoured him and were so honoured by him as no man thought he marched under the true banner of Mars that had not obtained Sir Philip Sidney's approbation. Men of affairs in most parts of Christendom entertained correspondency with him. But what speak I of these, with whom his own ways and ends did concur? since (to descend) his heart and capacity were so large that there was not a cunning painter, a skilful engineer, an excellent musician, or any other artificer of extraordinary fame, that made not himself known to this famous spirit and found him his true friend without hire and the common rendez-vous of worth in his time.

Now let princes vouchsafe to consider, of what importance it is to the honour of themselves and their estates to have one man of such eminence; not only as a nourisher of virtue in their courts or service, but besides for a reformed standard, by which even the most humorous persons could not but have a reverend ambition to be tried and approved current. This I do the more confidently affirm, because it will be confessed by all men that this one man's example and personal respect did not only encourage learning and honour in the schools, but brought the affection and true use thereof both into the court and camp. Nay more, even many gentlemen excellently learned amongst us will not deny but that they affected to row and steer their course in his wake. Besides which honour of unequal nature and education, his very ways in the world did generally add reputation to his prince and country, by restoring amongst us the ancient majesty of noble and true dealing: as a manly wisdom that can no more be weighed down by any effeminate craft than Hercules could be overcome by that contemptible army of dwarfs. This was it which, I profess, I loved dearly in him and still shall be glad to honour in the great men of this time: I mean that his heart and tongue went both one way, and so with everyone that went with the truth, as knowing no other kindred, party, or end.

Above all, he made the religion he professed the firm basis of his life: for this was his judgement (as he often told me) that our true-heartedness to the reformed religion in the beginning, brought peace, safety, and freedom to us; concluding that the wisest and best way was that of the famous William Prince of Orange, who never divided the consideration of estate from the cause of religion, nor gave that sound party occasion to be jealous or distracted upon any appearance of safety whatsoever; prudently resolving, that to temporize with the enemies of our faith was but (as among sea-gulls) a strife, not to keep upright, but aloft upon the top of every billow: which false-heartedness to God and man would in the end find itself forsaken of both, as Sir Philip conceived. For to this active spirit of his, all depths of the devil proved but shallow fords; he piercing into men's counsels and ends, not by their words, oaths, or compliments, all barren in that age, but by fathoming their hearts and powers by their deeds, and found no wisdom where he found no courage, nor courage without wisdom, nor either without honesty and truth. With which solid and active reaches of his, I am persuaded, he would have found or made a way through all the traverses even of the most weak and irregular times. But it pleased God in this decrepit age of the world, not to restore the image of her ancient vigour in him, otherwise than as in a lightning before death.

IV. THE EARL OF ESSEX

. . . having, in the earl's [Essex's] precipitate fortune curiously observed first, how long this nobleman's worth and favour had been flattered, tempted and stung by a swarm of sect-animals whose property was to wound and fly away, and so, by a continual affliction, probably enforce great hearts to turn and toss for ease, and in those passive postures perchance to tumble sometimes upon their sovereign's circles.

Into which pitfall of theirs, when they had once discerned this earl to be fallen, straight under the reverend style of Laesa Majestatis, all inferior ministers of justice (they knew) would be justly let loose to work upon him. And accordingly, under the same cloud, his enemies took audacity to cast libels abroad in his name against the state, made by themselves; set papers upon posts to bring his innocent friends in question. His power, by the jesuitical craft of rumour they made infinite, and his ambition more than equal to it. His letters to private men were read openly by the piercing eyes of an attorney's office which warranted the construction of every line in the worst sense against the writer.

Myself, his kinsman and, while I remained about the Queen, a kind of remora, staying the violent course of that fatal ship and these wind-watching passengers (at least as his enemies imagined), abruptly sent away to guard a figurative fleet, in danger of nothing but these prosopopeias of invisible rancour, and kept (as in a free prison) at Rochester till his head was off.

Before which sudden journey, casting mine eyes upon the catching court airs which I was to part from, I discerned my gracious sovereign to be every way so environed with these, not Jupiter's but Pluto's thunder-workers, as it was impossible for her to see any light that might lead to grace or mercy, but many encouraging meteors of severity as against an unthankful favourite and traitorous subject, he standing, by the law of England, condemned for such. So that let his heart be (as in my conscience it was) free from this unnatural crime, yet these un-returning steps seemed well worth the observing. Especially in the case of such a favourite as never put his sovereign to stand between her people and his errors, but here and abroad placed his body in the forefront against all that either threatened or assaulted her.

40   And being no admiral, nor yet a creator of admirals, whereby fear or hope might have kept those temporary Neptunes in a kind of subjection to him, yet he freely ventured himself in all sea-actions of his time. As if he would war the greatness of envy, place and power, with the greatness of worth and incomparable industry. Nevertheless he wanted not judgement to discern that whether they went with him or tarried behind, they must prob-ably prove unequal yoke-fellows in the one, or in the other passing curious and carping judges over all his public actions.

Again this gallant young earl, created (as it seems) for action,
50   before he was marshal, first as a private gentleman and after as a lieutenant by commission, went in the head of all our land troops that marched in his time; and, besides experience, still won ground even through competency, envy and confused mixtures of equality or inequality amongst the factious English, all inferior to his own active worth and merit.

Lastly, he was so far from affecting the absolute power of Henry III's favourites—I mean under a king to become equal, at least, with him in creating and deposing chancellors, treasurers and secretaries of state to raise a strong party for himself—as he
60   left both place and persons entire in their supreme jurisdictions or magistracies under his sovereign as she granted them. And though he foresaw a necessary diminution of their peaceful pre-dicaments by his carrying up the standard of Mars so high and withal knew that they, like wise men, must as certainly discern that the rising of his or falling of their scales depended upon the prosperity or unprosperity of his undertakings: yet, I say, that active heart of his freely chose to hazard himself upon their censures, without any other provisional rampier against the envious and suppressing crafts of that party than his own hope
70   and resolution to deserve well.

Neither did he (like the French favourites of that time) serve his own humours or necessities by selling seats of justice, nobility or orders of honour till they became *colliers pour toute bête*, to the disparagement of creating power and discouraging of the subject's hope or industry in attaining to advancement or profit: but suffered England to stand alone in her ancient degrees of freedoms and integrities, and so reserved that absolute power of creation sacred in his sovereign without any mercenary stain or alloy.

V. QUEEN ELIZABETH

. . . this blessed and blessing lady, with a calm mind as well in quiet as stirring times, studied how to keep her ancient under-earth buildings upon their first well-laid foundations. And if she found any strayed, rather to reduce them back to their original circuits than suffer a step to be made over or besides those time-authorised assemblies. And by this reservedness, ever coming upon the stage a commander and no petitioner, she preserved her state above the affronts of nobility or people, and, according to birthright, still became a sovereign judge over any dutiful or
10 encroaching petitions of nobles or commons.

For this lady, though not prophetically, yet like a provident princess, in the series of things and times foresaw through the long-lasting wisdom of government (a quintessence, howsoever abstracted out of moral philosophy and human laws, yet many degrees in use of mankind above them), she, I say, foresaw that every excess of passion expressed from the monarch, in acts or councils of estate would infallibly stir up in the people the like cobwebs of a popular spinning and therefore from these piercing grounds she concluded that a steady hand in the government of
20 sovereignty would ever prove more prosperous than any nimble or witty practice, crafty shifting, or imperious forcing humours possibly could do.

Again in the latitude which some modern princes allow to their favourites as supporters of government and middle walls between power and the people's envy, it seems this Queen reservedly kept entrenched within her native strengths and sceptre.

For even in the height of Essex his credit with her, how far was she from permitting him (like a Remus) to leap over any wall of her new-built Anti-Rome; or with a young and inexperienced genius to shuffle pulpits, parliaments, laws and other fundamental establishments of her kingdoms into any glorious appearances of will or power? It should seem foreseeing that howsoever this unexpected racking of people might for a time in some particulars both please and add a glossy stick to enlarge the eagle's nest, yet that in the end all buildings above the truth must necessarily have forced her two supremacies of state and nature to descend and through irregularities acted in her name either become a sanctuary between the world and inferior persons' errors; or (as playing an after-game with her subjects, for a subject) constrain her to change the tenure of commanding power into a kind of unprincely mediation. And for what? Even vainly to entreat her people that they would hope well of diverse confusions, howsoever they might seem heady, nay ignorant passions and such as threatened no less than a loss of native liberties descended upon her people by the same prescription of time and right by which the crown had descended upon herself and her ancestors; with a probable consequence of many more sharp-pointed tyrannies over them and their freedoms than their happily deceased parents ever tasted or dreamed of.

Besides, admit these flatterings and threatenings of hope or fear (which transcendent power is sometimes forced to work by) could have drawn this excellent princess and her time-present subjects to make brass an equally current standard with gold or silver within her sea-compassed dominions, yet abroad, where the freedom of other sovereignties is bounded by religion, justice, and well-weighed commerce amongst neighbour-princes, she foresaw the least thought of multiplying self-prerogatives there would instantly be discredited and reflected back to stir up discouragement in the softest hearts of her most humble and dutiful subjects.

Therefore, contrary to all these captived and captiving appearances, this experienced governess of ours published to the world, by a constant series in her actions, that she never was, nor ever would be, overloaden with any such excesses in her person or defects in her government as might constrain her to support or be supported by a monopolous use of favourites; as if she would make any greater than herself, to govern tyrannically by them.

VI. GREVILLE'S BEGINNINGS IN POETRY

When my youth, with favour of court in some moderate proportion to my birth and breeding, in the activeness of that time gave
me opportunity of most business, then did my yet undiscouraged
genius most affect to find or make work for itself. And out of that
freedom, having many times offered my fortune to the course of
foreign employments as the properest forges to fashion a subject
for the real services of his sovereign, I found the returns of those
mis-placed endeavours to prove both a vain charge to myself and
an offensive undertaking to that excellent governess over all her
10 subjects' duties and affections. . . .

By which many warnings, I finding the specious fires of youth
to prove far more scorching than glorious, called my second
thoughts to council, and in that map clearly discerning action and
honour to fly with more wings than one, and that it was sufficient
for the plant to grow where his sovereign's hand had planted it, I
found reason to contract my thoughts from those larger but
wandering horizons of the world abroad, and bound my prospect
within the safe limits of duty, in such home services as were
acceptable to my sovereign.

20 In which retired view, Sir Philip Sidney, that exact image of
quiet and action, happily united in him and seldom well divided
in any, being ever in mine eyes, made me think it no small degree
of honour to imitate or tread in the steps of such a leader. So that
to sail by his compass was shortly (as I said) one of the principal
reasons I can allege which persuaded me to steal minutes of
time from my daily services, and employ them in this kind of
writing.

VII. GREVILLE'S COMMENTS ON HIS OWN WORKS

The works (as you see) are tragedies, with some treatises annexed.
The treatises (to speak truly of them) were first intended to be for
every Act a chorus, and though not born out of the present matter
acted, yet being the largest subjects I could then think upon, and
no such strangers to the scope of the tragedies but that a favourable
reader might easily find some consanguinity between them: I,

preferring this general scope of profit before the self-reputation of being an exact artisan in that poetical mystery, conceived that a perspective into vice, and the unprosperities of it, would prove more acceptable to every good reader's ends, than any bare murmur of discontented spirits against their present government, or horrible periods of exorbitant passions among equals.

Which with humble sails after I had once ventured upon this spreading ocean of images, my apprehensive youth, for lack of a well touched compass, did easily wander beyond proportion. And in my old age again, looking back on them with a father's eye: when I considered first, how poorly the inward natures of those glorious names were expressed: then how much easier it was to excuse deformities, than to cure them; though I found reason to change their places, yet I could not find in my heart to bestow cost or care in altering their light and limited apparel in verse. . . .

Now for the several branches, or discourses following: they are all members of one and the same imperfect body, so as I let them take their fortunes (like essays) only to tempt and stir up some more free genius, to fashion the whole frame into finer mould for the world's use. . . .

Lastly concerning the tragedies themselves: they were in their first creation three, whereof Antony and Cleopatra, according to their irregular passions in forsaking empire to follow sensuality, were sacrificed to the fire. The executioner, the author himself. Not that he conceived it to be a contemptible younger brother to the rest, but lest, while he seemed to look over much upward, he might stumble into the astronomer's pit. Many members in that creature (by the opinion of those few eyes which saw it) having some childish wantonness in them, apt enough to be construed or strained to a personating of vices in the present governors and government.

From which cautious prospect, I bringing into my mind the ancient poet's metamorphosing man's reasonable nature into the sensitive of beasts or vegetative of plants; and knowing these all (in their true moral) to be but images of the unequal balance between humours and times, nature and place; and again in the practice of the world, seeing the like instance not poetically, but really, fashioned in the Earl of Essex then falling, and ever till then worthily beloved, both of Queen and people: this sudden descent of such greatness, together with the quality of the actors in every scene, stirred up the author's second thoughts to be careful (in his own case) of leaving fair weather behind him. . . .

50   Now to return to the tragedies remaining: my purpose in them was, not (with the ancient) to exemplify the disastrous miseries of man's life, where order, laws, doctrine, and authority are unable to protect innocency from the exorbitant wickedness of power, and so out of that melancholic vision, stir horror or murmur against Divine Providence; nor yet (with the modern) to point out God's revenging aspect upon every particular sin, to the despair or confusion of mortality; but rather to trace out the high ways of ambitious governors, and to show in the practice, that the more audacity, advantage, and good success such sovereignties have, the more they hasten to their own desolation and ruin.

60   So that to this abstract end, finding all little instruments in discovery of great bodies to be seldom without errors, I presumed, or it rather escaped me, to make my images beyond the ordinary stature of excess, wherein again that women are predominant is not for malice, or ill talent to their sex; but as poets figured the virtues to be women and all nations call them by feminine names, so have I described malice, craft, and such like vices in the persons of shrews, to show that many of them are of that nature, even as we are, I mean strong in weakness, and consequently in these orbs of passion, the weaker sex commonly the most predominant; yet as I 70   have not made all women good with Euripides, so have I not made them all evil with Sophocles, but mixed of such sorts as we find both them, and ourselves.

Again, for the arguments of these tragedies they be not naked and casual like the Greek and Latin, nor (I confess) contrived with the variety and unexpected encounters of the Italians, but nearer levelled to those humours, counsels, and practises, wherein I thought fitter to hold the attention of the reader, than in the strangeness or perplexedness of witty fictions, in which the affections, or imagination, may perchance find exercise and 80   entertainment but the memory and judgement no enriching at all; besides, I conceived these delicate images to be over-abundantly furnished in all languages already.

And though my noble friend had that dexterity, even with the dashes of his pen to make the Arcadian antiques beautify the

margins of his works; yet the honour which (I bear him record) he never affected, I leave unto him, with this addition, that his end in them was not vanishing pleasure alone, but moral images and examples, (as directing threads) to guide every man through the confused labyrinth of his own desires and life: so that how-
90   soever I liked them too well (even in that unperfected shape they were) to condescend that such delicate (though inferior) pictures of himself should be suppressed; yet I do wish that work may be the last in this kind, presuming no man that follows can ever reach, much less go beyond, that excellent intended pattern of his.

For my own part, I found my creeping genius more fixed upon the images of life than the images of wit and therefore chose not to write to them on whose foot the black ox had not already trod, as the proverb is, but to those only that are weather-beaten in the sea of this world, such as having lost the sight of their gardens and
100   groves, study to sail on a right course among rocks and quick-sands; and if in thus ordaining, and ordering matter and form together for the use of life, I have made those tragedies no plays for the stage, be it known, it was no part of my purpose to write for them, against whom so many good and great spirits have already written.

But he that will behold these Acts upon their true stage, let him look on that stage wherein himself is an actor, even the state he lives in, and for every part he may perchance find a player, and for every line (it may be) an instance of life, beyond the author's
110   intention or application, the vices of former ages being so like to these of this age as it will be easy to find out some affinity or resemblance between them, which whosoever readeth with this apprehension, will not perchance think the scenes too large, at least the matter not to be exceeded in account of words.

Lastly, for the style: as it is rich or poor according to the estate and ability of the writer, so the value of it shall be enhanced or cried down according to the grace and the capacity of the reader; from which common fortune of books, I look for no exemption.

But to conclude, as I began this work to entertain and instruct
120   myself, so if any other find entertainment or profit by it, let him use it freely, judge honourably of my friend, and moderately of me, which is all the return that out of this barren stock can be desired or expected.

NOTES

CAELICA

Some of the poems or parts of poems were set to music by contemporary composers. Of those chosen in this selection, such are:

Nos. 1, 2, 3, 26, 27, 28 (first 2 sts. only), 31, set by Martin Peerson in *Mottects or Grave Chamber Musique,* 1630.

No. 1 also set by Michael Cavendish in *Ayres in Tabletorie,* 1598.

No. 14 set by John Dowland in *First Booke of Songes and Ayres,* 1597.

1 (I) A skilfully patterned poem, of substance as well as artifice. The last two lines repeat the key words of st. 1 with the effect of summarising and clinching the argument of the poem.

2 (III) A lover's image of his heart as the temple in which the mistress is worshipped. Greville keeps the serious values of the religious references in view throughout.

1–2. Cf. the neo-platonic idea that beauty and love emanate from God and their earthly embodiments lead the soul to the Divine. The opening lines of Spenser's *Amoretti* VIII are very close to Greville's: 'More than most fair, full of the living fire, Kindled above unto the maker near'. **5–6.** Images were defaced at the Reformation. **7.** *Window of the sky.* The lady's beauty is a means by which heavenly beauty can be glimpsed.

3 (IV) Comparison of the lady's eyes to stars is a commonplace of love poetry but Greville handles the convention with a difference. St. 1 uses astrological language to compare the influence of the celestial bodies on men's lives and minds with that of the lady's eyes, while St. 2 uses theological language and applies it, as sonnet *2* (III) does to the lady.

2. *Apollo.* The Sun. **3.** *aspects.* Relative positions of the planets as they appear to an observer on earth. **10.** Reason and Affection (i.e. Passion) were usually opposed, as in Sidney's *Astrophil and Stella* 18. Cf. The Chorus Sacerdotum of *Mustapha:* 'Passion and Reason, self-division cause'. **14.** *election.* Choosing, with a reference to the Puritan doctrine that the soul is saved not by faith or good works but by Divine Grace.

4 (X) This poem continues the idea of *2* (III) that the beloved is an image of divine beauty and the poet argues that she should be worshipped as an ideal rather than wooed as a mortal woman. For the purposes of this poem he envisages Love as a separable part of the mind, and he recounts how it has been inspired to seek the beloved but has proved incapable of the kind of unselfish devotion which should be offered to ideal beauty and virtue. As a consequence Love has fallen, as the angels fell from heaven. The second stanza paints a powerful picture of the mind as the hell it may become if it is not purified and exalted by devotion to something superior to itself. In the third stanza Love is bidden to return to the lady, to learn to contemplate her perfections and to renounce selfish desire.

5–6. Greville suggests vanity, a divided will, or the overwhelming beauty and virtue of his mistress as reasons why his love has retired from her service. **10.** *Wit*. Wit should create ideas but now merely imitates (seeks resemblances). **15.** *you divine*. Do you foresee (expect)? **21–4.** The Platonic ideals alone should be worshipped, not their earthly embodiments. Greville combines this idea with the Protestant one that to worship the saints instead of God is idolatry.

5 (XI) Juno, angry because Jove has been unfaithful to her with Io, determines to banish Cupid to a cold climate (i.e. Britain) where he will not be so dangerous. The poem ends with a piece of sardonic psychology: desire once kindled in the sexually repressed, lust and shame feed upon each other till both grow exorbitant and insatiable. In *Astrophil and Stella* 8 Sidney handles a similar Cupid story very differently.

3. *equinoctial*. Lands near the equator. **6.** A reference to coal fires? **14** *still*. Always.

6 (XVIII) Caelica complains on the one hand that her lover is unfaithful to her and on the other that he is too weakly devoted. In the last part of the sestet he returns the charge of ill conduct upon her. The difference in tone between this poem and no. *4* (X), from the ideal and figurative to the dramatic and realistic, is striking.

7 (XXI) A witty and sophisticated poem about women's duplicity. St. 1 explains why there are no sailors in hell. **5–8.** The satyr baffled by the shepherd's blowing both hot and cold appears in the 22nd fable of Avyan and in G. Whitney's *Choice of Emblems*, 1586, p. 160.

8 (XXII) Unlike no. *7* (XXI), *8* (XXII) has a deceptive air of simplicity. The first three stanzas charmingly describe a rural wooing but the mythological allusions of st. 4 prepare for the accusation at the end that Myra was never as innocent as she seemed but was smoothing the way for future unfaithfulness by refusing ever to express her love in writing.

2. *Ware*. Wore. **3–4.** His name was written in soot on the chimney back. **12.** Myra distributes her love favours to many, as five thousand were fed by loaves and fishes. **19.** Argus, who had a hundred eyes, was a guardian set to keep watch on behalf of Juno (Jove's wife) over Io, one of Jove's loves: perhaps here it is Myra's nurse or mother who is on watch against a lover. **24.** Venus, wife of Vulcan, took Mars as her lover and Vulcan ensnared them in a net as they lay together. *Vulcan's brothers*. Myra's more favoured suitors. In the myth, the husband ensnared his wife and her lover in order to shame them; but in this situation the favoured lovers, enjoying a husband's privileges, exclude a rival from the pleasures they enjoy.

9 (XXXVI) Greville's political observations reinforce his criticism of the pretended innocence of women.

1–4. The king can do no wrong: therefore as a child the prince has whipping boys who are punished for his faults, and later his ministers bear the brunt of his mistakes. **13–14.** No scholarship has yet been able to determine whether bad or weak kings are the worse.

10 (XXXIX) Men built the tower of Babel (*Genesis* 11, 1–9), thinking that it might touch heaven, and the lover aspired to possess Caelica's heart, which is heaven to him. The men of Babylon were punished for their over-weening pride by confusion of tongues and the poet meets a similar fate when Caelica refuses to grant him sympathetic understanding. The language of the poem plays characteristically between secular and religious references.

6. They thought they could change their places in the order of things by exercising craft.

11 (XL) An attractive sonnet on the theme of time and beauty. The image of the ripening wheat may remind us of Greville's close associations with the Warwickshire countryside. The use of feminine rhymes gives a touch of melancholy and the transience of beauty is hinted at in l.13.

1. *nurse-life.* Life-sustaining. **4.** The sight of the growing wheat makes the labour of cultivation pleasurable. **12.** Love and Glory were united in her early beauty like two lovers in marriage. **13.** In her maturity her love-inspiring beauty is at its peak, as the sun is at its height at noon. There is a suggestion of the *carpe diem* idea. **14.** Caelica's beauty draws men's desires to her as the heat of the sun draws up moisture from the earth.

12 (XLIV) The first 2 sts. describe the lost golden age of abundance and innocence celebrated in a famous chorus 'O bella età de l'oro' in Tasso's *Aminta*. Guarini imitated this in *Il Pastor Fido* and Greville also seems to be recalling Tasso. St. 3 contrasts this golden world with the enfeebled and corrupt present. The last st. weaves a complex web of allusions round these ideas. The reference (**13–16**) to 'a wavering province' and to a change from monarchy to oligarchy, seen as a change for the worse, has political associations. There is an astrological reference (**17–18**) as Saturn is identified not only with the mythical ruler of the golden age but also with the planet, and mention of the other planets recalls the gods, led by Jove (Jupiter), who overthrew Saturn. Beneath these images of disorder and dissolution, Caelica is being described. No longer beautiful, or young, or faithful, she has changed one lover for perhaps several others. The old lover thinks he has little to regret. The poem, beginning within a conventional framework, becomes an attack upon the mistress which is not the less ruthless for being couched in ostensibly impersonal terms.

6. Beauty was then neither a snare nor was it artificial. **9.** The four ages of man are gold, silver, bronze (here 'brazen' with perhaps the suggestion of shamelessness) and iron. Cf. Ovid, *Metamorphoses* bk. I. **17.** *gilt age.* Golden age.

13 (L) Evidently a jest-book tale, though it is not in the extant (1626) edition of the *Jests of Scoggin* (Edward IV's fool). The anecdote goes back to Giovanni the Florentine's *Il Pecorone* (1558) where it is included in a cruel tale about a husband's punishment of his unfaithful wife.

8. Jove visited Danae in a shower of gold and she became the mother of Perseus. Greville means that the lord had sexual intercourse with the woman and also gave her money.

14 (LII) A cheerfully cynical song about love as a careless pleasure.

17–18. When love and honour pull against each other, miracles of devotion and restraint may be achieved. **21–2.** If she is no longer faithful to him he will not make much of the loss but dismiss it as a mere trifle. **24.** The cuckoo is traditionally associated with adultery. **27.** As set to music by Dowland and in a version of the poem in the Arundel ms., this line reads 'And love as well the foster can', i.e. the forester can love as well as the nobleman. The WF text may be paraphrased: 'Love can cherish you as effectively as money and power.'

15 (LVI) The sentiments of this poem are at the opposite pole from those of no. *4* (X) where the poet bade his love 'in contemplation feed desire'.

24. Vulcan was Venus's husband (cf. *8*. l. 24): Cynthia was probably married. **25–48.** These lines occur in the Warwick ms. but are omitted from the edition of 1633. **36.** *Thetis.* A sea-goddess. When the sun rises above the horizon at sea as if it were coming out of the water. **38.** *Apollo.* God of the sun. **40.** *Aurora.* Goddess of the dawn. **45–8.** Phaeton, son of the sun god, was allowed to drive the chariot of the sun across the skies for one day but he came so near the earth as nearly to set it on fire. **62.** *line.* Equator. **71.** By a common Elizabethan *double entendre*, 'to die' refers to orgasm in sexual intercourse.

16 (LVIII) A curious poem about Caelica's use of a golden wig when she was young, and rejection of it now she is old. The intention may be simply to pay a rather bizarre compliment to the memory of Caelica's charms when young, but there seems to be a vein of irony in the poem.

1. *springs.* Shoots, young growth. **7–8.** Blonde beauty was the conventional ideal: see Shakespeare's flouting of the convention in sonnet CXXX. **18.** *thoughts.* Minds and hearts.

17 (LIX) The danger facing those who sail to find a fortune in America is used as an allegory of the experiences of the lover. The strength of the language suggests that Greville recognises that both the search for El Dorado and the pursuit of a mistress's love may be images of spiritual experience in search of God. The Bermudas were notorious for their storms. Raleigh described 'the sea about the Bermudas' as 'a hellish sea of thunder, lightning and storms' (*Discovery of the large, rich and beautiful Empire of Guiana*) and Shakespeare's *Tempest* draws on accounts of a shipwreck there in 1609.

18 (LX) Greville gives a typically thoughtful treatment to his mistress's reproaches to him for his love of privacy. Cf. the much more extrovert treatment of the theme in *Astrophil and Stella* 27.

4. *self-respect.* Egoism.

19 (LXI) His love is dead beyond reviving and he suggests that Caelica should console herself with somebody else. The variety and vivacity of the illustrations by which he tries to convince her of the hopelessness of trying to restore his love make it an attractive poem. The apparently careless lover makes some penetrating observations. The poem is composed of alternating 4- and 6-lined sts.

19–20. Some mountains sometimes move i.e. by landslides, and love is sometimes constant, but both these phenomena are rare. **31–2.** If we insist on remembering the past in the present, we shall much resent the changes made by time. **46–7.** It is a foolish indulgence of self-pity to complain of a lost love, for there is nothing to be done about it. **48.** Avenge yourself for your lover's unfaithfulness by betraying someone else. **49–50.** Faithfulness when love is not returned is mere drudgery. When the love is reciprocated faithfulness will be esteemed differently.

20 (LXVI) All human learning embodied in books is corrupted by the consequences of man's fall. Real truths are taught when men learn from experience, and with revealed truth as their guide, the nature of good and evil. The ideas expressed in the poem are very close to those of the first sixty stanzas of *A Treaty of Human Learning* where also Greville discredits the pretensions of purely human learning. In the treatise he goes on to distinguish some of the ways in which human arts, suitably chastened, may, in spite of their imperfections, be useful, but in the *Caelica* poem he does nothing to soften the sharpness of the opposition between the specious and sinful products of human endeavour and the real wisdom of the spiritually pure.

12. Ixion embraced a phantom, believing it to be the goddess Juno and so engendered the centaurs, hybrid creatures, half horses, half men. **20.** *thorough.* Through, i.e. by means of. **27.** It is not from some accidental cause that we are ignorant, but because of innate corruption of our nature. **32.** *in the serving rooms.* i.e. as servants. **40-2.** The regenerate man renounces the desires and pride of the flesh and an image of divine truth, which was lost at the fall, forms again in his mind. Revealed truth speaks of God's miraculous dealings with the world. **45.** *Methods.* Systematic treatises.

21 (LXIX) When cycles of history come to an end, there are great disturbances in the usual order of things. In the same way, changes in love produce unnatural situations in which values are reversed.

1. *this All.* The universe. **2.** *revolution.* The turning of the planets through a complete circuit or course. The completion of the cycle was thought to cause upheavals on earth. **9.** *overthwart.* Thwarted. **15.** Greville uses the idea that men on the other side of the world 'walk upside down' in another *Caelica* poem: 'The feet of men against our feet do move' (LXIII). The use of it in no. *21* (LXIX) is figurative, to indicate that his mistress now favours his rivals.

22 (LXXI) Cupid's escapades provided a popular range of material for sonneteers, but this poem strikes unusually deep notes. Ostensibly it tells of the poet's rejection by an ungrateful mistress but his language suggests a further level of significance. St. 3 compares truth to a mistress with faith to God. God's faithful may have to accept shame and misery in the world as the badge of their allegiance. The lover's fall from his paradise in the mistress's heart is compared to Adam's fall, but whereas Adam fell through knowledge of sin, the lover, though he inherits Adam's world, did not understand that human relationships are vitiated as a result of the fall. If the language implies that devotion which should be God's is bound to meet with disillusion when offered to an earthly object, Cupid seems not entirely to have learnt this lesson. He suggests knowledge, honour, fame, as suitable objects of his service, but in other poems these, as much as sexual love, are described as flawed by human corruption.

2. *seisin and livery.* A formula implying legal possession. There are legal images also in **3, 8,** and **13.**

23 (LXXIV) Two constant lovers meet after a time of separation. The poem traces the man's reading of the changing expressions on the woman's face as he wonders whether he dare make love to her. In the end he refrains for fear of offending her and the poet comments that he should have been more bold.

22. *fet.* Fetch. **45-6.** Cynthia may be taken as the goddess of chastity, but it is also one of the names given to the mistress in these poems. Two of the names given to the woman occur in this poem (Caelica and Myra) so it is possible that the third is used as well. If Cynthia is the woman, the lines mean: he thinks that her movements of withdrawal, as if in fear, are merely to satisfy her own scruples. **55–6.** The moon-goddess (Cynthia) kissed Endymion as he slept on a hill, but it is not likely in the present instance that the woman will make all the advances.

Both W and F give a confused presentation of this poem. F takes ll. 55–62 as a separate poem and W treats ll. 25–62 as separate.

24 (LXXVII) The relation of princes to the law was one of the tenderest subjects in contemporary thought and it is the subject of one section of Greville's treatise *Of Monarchy*. There he is concerned with aspects of government in which the politic and expedient play a large part. In the *Caelica* poem he makes an unequivocal statement of his judgement that kings have craftily wrested the law to serve their own purposes and to enslave their people.

7. Time and human selfishness substitute artificial codes of conduct for natural merit. **10–12.** Under cover of the pretence that thrones are subject to law, kings encroach upon the people's freedom to an intolerable extent. **13–14.** Judges allow kings to administer as well as to expound the law. **16.** Laws become the instruments of power. **17.** *with equal shows*. Equality before the law is only a pretence. **28.** Gradual encroachments are made on subjects' liberties so that the people are ensnared, as in a spider's web, by threads almost imperceptible, but not to be escaped.

25 (LXXVIII) An attack on unworthy court favourites and on monarchs who cultivate them. This is one of the preoccupations of Greville's *Life of Sidney*, written during the reign of James I.

3. Jet has magnetic power upon straws. **6.** *staple-rate*. The rate appropriate for the most important commodities of a state. **8.** *erect*. Build; do anything constructive. **17–18.** They are elevated to high positions but present only a show of authority and nobility: they have no real merit. **20.** *stale*. Decoy-bird. **24.** The reference is to the fable of the wren who won a race by sitting on an eagle's back. Men may deprive themselves of real power to become dependent upon another's. **25–6.** A dog carrying meat in his mouth sees himself reflected in water, snaps at his reflection, and loses the meat he is carrying. This is the 5th fable of the first book of Aesop's fables.

26 (LXXXI) In praise of Queen Elizabeth.

1. *Under a throne*. Under the canopy of a throne. **3.** *guards*. The word has the usual sense of guardians and is also an astronomical term referring to two stars in the constellation Ursa Minor, often used for navigation. **5.** The homage paid her is not the product of mere calculation. **8.** *unobserving*. Not observing decorum, the proper conduct of affairs.

27 (LXXXIV) The poet turns from the service of Cupid to the service of God. There are no more love poems in the sequence and religious themes predominate from this point on.

9–11. These lines, like others earlier in the sequence, describe a love situation in language which has religious reference. The primary meaning is: he did not seek love only for the sake of having children nor did he expect Cupid to mend his ways and always ensure him kind treatment. He was willing to expect alternate hope and fear to be the story of his life. The resonance of the phrase 'I bowed not to thy image' and the words 'reformed' and 'confession' suggest, however, how misguided it is to devote a life to Cupid and the folly of it is made plain in **12**.

14. Cf. Sidney's 'Leave me, O love, which reachest but to dust And thou my mind aspire to higher things'.

28 (LXXXV) This poem defines the higher love to which the poet has now committed himself. Compare no. *4* (x). Love is no longer erotic desire tempered by Platonic idealism but a spiritual quality, beautifully described in the first two quatrains.

13–14. Glory is an attribute of the eternal; to ascribe it to anything else is to misrepresent its true nature.

29 (LXXXVI) Man's physical existence and his inner life are both subject to disturbance and distress. We should not be offended (distasted) with the physical heavens because our earth suffers natural calamities. Similarly we should not blame heaven for our moral and spiritual woes. Resignation and fortitude may teach us endurance, but, better than this, if we surrender ourselves utterly to God, the human condition will be transcended. To enforce his parallel between the inner and outer conditions of men, Greville uses the same rhyme words throughout the octave of this sonnet. All the rhymes in the poem have feminine endings but the extra-metrical syllables of the couplet are given weight and this serves to give special emphasis to the final lines.

30 (LXXXVII) The poem ensivages the terrors of death to those who take no thought for repentance during their life.

11–12. The 'living men' may well be in the same position as the man about whom they enquire.

31 (LXXXVIII) The pursuit of vain knowledge is contrasted with the supreme need for spiritual rebirth.

6. Curiosity about such topics gives sin opportunities to work. **9.** Cf. no. *10* (XXXIX). **11.** *the Law.* Like Calvin, Greville understands the Law in a wide sense: 'By that word "Law", I mean not only the ten precepts which show us the rule of righteous and holy living, but the form of religion as God published it by the hand of Moses' (Calvin, *The Institutes of the Christian Religion*, Bk. 2, chap. 7, 1). **12.** *types.* Persons, objects or events of Old Testament history, prefiguring the revelations of the New. The regenerate man will find former experience quite superseded. **13.** *swept the house.* Cleansed the heart and mind. **15–16.** When the individual life is sanctified by God's grace, there is a miraculous transformation of wordly experience. **17.** Only goodness is capable of comprehending God.

32 (LXXXIX) The duties of a Christian life are not discharged simply by having a refined understanding of the nature of Christ's sacrifice: the sacrifice of our own earthly nature is required before we can claim salvation.

1–6. Idols do not have to be 'without' i.e. external, tangible objects: they may also be mental. Greville gives as an example the Manicheans who, he says, concentrated on a mental image of Christ's crucifixion when they wished to pray. The idea of 'idols' of the mind, false images which distract from the real truth, recalls Bacon's famous account of the varieties of such idols in *Novum Organum*. **11–12.** It is living by one's faith that matters, not a purely verbal profession.

33 (XCI) In this poem, as in others of the *Caelica* sequence, Greville makes a firm judgement of themes which occupy him at greater length in other poems. *An Inquisition upon Fame and Honour* is the title of one of his verse treatises and *A Treatise of Monarchy* contains a section 'Of Nobility'. In the longer poems, though his sense of absolutes remains the same, Greville allows some practical value to concepts of fame and honour and assesses nobility as a useful instrument of government. In *Caelica* he dismisses all these things without qualification as nothing but reflections of man's vanity and perverted sense of values.

7-12. Wise kings, by conferring nobility, gild the chains by which they bind those who serve them. This, though they are none the less subject, makes them accept their subjection more happily.

34 (xciv) Greville's illustrations of his point seem to reflect his experience of state office (he was treasurer of the navy from 1598-1603, and he became chancellor of the exchequer in 1614) and also his knowledge of life in the countryside.

2. *tellers.* Four officers of the exchequer charged with the receipt or payment of moneys. **4.** *Black hands.* Because they handled coins. **5-6.** When tax-collecting and other duties are well carried out and supervised, nobody will love the tax-collectors. (The idea is, perhaps, that they will not take bribes but press the law to the limit.)

35 (xcvii) A more urgent statement of the point of no. *32* (lxxxix): that lip-service to Christ's teaching is not enough.

19. *Sodom . . . Lot.* See *Genesis* 19. **20.** Treat God's laws and gospel as if they were so much matter for intellectual ingenuity to play upon. **22.** We have not yet come to the end of our impiety.

36 (xcviii) A subtle poem in which Greville analyses his state of sin. Cf. Donne's *A Hymn to God the Father*.

7. *never comprehended.* Never encompassed, i.e. without limit. **16.** He must repent of sinning against God, not because he fears the punishment that sin will bring.

37 (xcix) The first 2 sts. describe the state of hell into which man is plunged when he realises the horror of his sins. Those without faith fall into despair but the last 2 sts. tell how to the believer, when his unworthiness most weighs upon him, the grace of God is offered. In st. 3, God defeats the negatives of hell and sin by opposing to them power, truth, glory and bounty ('unprivation') and in st. 4, the vicarious atonement of Christ releases the sinful soul from hell. The use of a refrain, with the slight but important variant in sts. 3 and 4, is very effective.

38 (cviii) Greville writes on war in section xii of *A Treatise of Monarchy* and also in *A Treaty of Wars*. In the *Caelica* poem he gives a very condensed and subtle treatment of some of his thoughts on the subject. Peace is the nurse of many abuses and war, on the other hand, has specious attractions. Two quatrains follow three 6-lined sts. and the poem ends with another st. of 6 lines.

7-12. The idea that war is a healthy purgative of corrupt humours is a recurrent one. Cf. Tennyson's *Maud*. **13-18.** In peace power tyrannises till it excites revolt in abused subjects who claim the legal rights which are being denied them. **31-2.** There is a double image in these lines, of the phoenix which consumes itself in fire only to be re-born, and of the martyrs who perished at the stake for their faith. The second seems the stronger image in the context. Heroes in war are martyrs to fame and power and honour. Greville asks whether their sacrifice is worthwhile and the weighting of the language strongly implies that it is not.

39 (CIX) A call for the Last Judgement, that the sins of the world may be swept away.

15–18. The contrast between institutional religion and the inner light is a recurrent point whenever Greville writes of the church. **17.** *them that seem thine own.* The clergy. **19–24** are omitted in the Warwick ms.

THE TREATISES

Greville began to work on the poems which eventually took shape as the treatises at an early stage of his writing career, but he seems to have revised them extensively at various periods thereafter. In the *Life of Sidney* he gives an account of the kind of revisions to *A Treatise of Monarchy* which he had made up to the time of writing, but the full history of the successive developments of this and of the other treatises cannot be traced on the evidence at present available. They are all deeply thoughtful poems and represent Greville's continuing attempt, over many years, to fashion into succinct and pithy verse his assessment of men's political and personal natures and also his judgement of these in relation to God's claims to repentance and obedience. The dense and compressed character of the verse produces difficulties, but most of them yield with familiarity.

A TREATISE OF MONARCHY

Stanzas 27–33 In these sts. from near the beginning of the treatise, Greville sets the relation between monarch and subject in the context of his thinking about human life in general. Since kings and subjects alike share the frailty of fallen human nature, they should not expect too much of each other. They should take a practical view of their mutual relations and settle them on the basis of law and custom and a recognition of human limitations.

9. *touch.* Distinguishing quality. **10.** Neither has any certain knowledge about his duties, capacities or desires. **24.** *misprision.* Misjudgement, perhaps scorn of, the other party. **33.** *peising.* Weighing. *scales of grace.* Religious values. **35.** Abstract notions of philosophy.

Stanzas 106–14 These are of particular interest for two reasons. The description of those who 'disgraced live, restrained, or not used' (**28**) seems to point to Greville's own situation during the years between 1604 and 1614 when he was out of office. His refusal to accept permanent retirement and his willingness later to work with James I and with the Duke of Buckingham seem to be reflections of the philosophy advanced here: that it is one's duty, however uncongenial the circumstances, to work to achieve the best possible. In the second place, though rebellion is not the topic here, these lines imply an attitude to the debate which exercised many thinkers of his day: was it legitimate for the subject to rebel if the monarch abused his powers and privileges and became tyrannical? Calvin taught non-resistance in all circumstances to lawfully constituted authority since kings are responsible to God alone. John Knox, on the other hand, affirmed that it was the duty of the godly to resist, by force if necessary, the rule of an impious monarch. Greville's answer to the despair which may overtake a man living under unrighteous rulers (**38–56**) is that no human situations endure for ever, that God controls the revolutions of time, and that men should wait for the bad times to pass. In other words, his political analysis of the respective duties of monarch and subject is in the last resort subordinated to his overall view of the vanity and transience of earthly things. For an account of the religious and political arguments advanced by contemporary thinkers, see J. W. Allen, *A History of Political Thought in the Sixteenth Century* (especially pp. 52–60 and 103–20) and H. N. Maclean, 'Fulke Greville: Kingship and Sovereignty', *Huntington Library Quarterly*, xvi (1953), 237–271.

1–2. *those declinations . . . estate.* The immediately preceding sts. describe changes which in the course of time bring states from greatness to ruin. **11–12.** God is the First Cause. *ghostly physic.* Spiritual healing. **19–23.** Lucius Annaeus Seneca was Nero's tutor and later his counsellor. Among the victims of Nero's cruelty were his own brother, Britannicus, and his mother, Agrippina. **23–4.** In the height of storms, sea pilots give up their skills as useless and abandon themselves to fate. **32.** *equality.* Equability. **35.** Neratius Priscus lived through the tyrannical reign of Domitian and became a jurist of note under Trajan and Hadrian. **39.** After the death of Pompey, Cato the Stoic committed suicide rather than live under Caesar.

Stanzas 409–12 These stanzas bring together three Elizabethan motifs, patriotism, fear of the Turkish menace, and concern with sea power. Greville himself had a personal interest in the navy of which he was treasurer in the last years of Elizabeth's reign. He had quite considerable experience of ships and was made rear-admiral in 1599 and given command of a ship in a fleet prepared to meet an expected Spanish invasion. His writings are full of images of the sea and sailing.

7–12. The references are to the defeat of the Persian fleet at Salamis in 480 B.C. and the defeat of the Turkish fleet at Lepanto in 1571. **17.** *wall.* Shakespeare uses the same image in *Richard II*, II i., 47: 'Which serves it in the office of a wall'.

A TREATY OF HUMAN LEARNING

14. *succeed.* Follow in order. **16.** *move but not remove.* Poetry and music can stir men's emotions but not effect decisive changes in their behaviour. **18.** *mend . . . it.* Improve the condition of our life. **34–9.** Poetry created on foundations of truth adds beauty to truth. Though such poetry appears to be merely delightful, in fact, by the orderly disposition of the words and ideas, it teaches how to observe order and proportion in our lives. **45.** Teaches and creates, but cannot compel.

A TREATISE OF RELIGION

1. Greville has been explaining how God helps those who struggle to overcome sin and to attain salvation. **4.** Christ demands of us only faith and obedience. **8.** Pomp is a growth from the root of power: the growth will be pruned and the root itself may be dug up. **13-18.** *arts.* All kinds of skills, and all efforts of human intelligence to construct systems and methodologies. Since arts involve sophistication, Greville's use of the word very often associates them with man's over-weening pride in his own capacities and the contamination of what is pure and straightforward. 'Riddles of the sin' brings together both ideas. The primal sin ('*the* sin') which all men inherit is pride, and clever men who seek to impose upon others for their own self-gratification cloak the skills by which they manage men and affairs in obscurity, so that they can operate more securely. 'Riddles' also implies that those who rely on human skills and intelligence alone will never perceive the plain truth but will lose themselves in unprofitable puzzles. **25.** *speculation.* Sight, vision. **37-42.** Greville always excepts from his strictures upon humanity certain 'pure souls' who, by special grace, really live according to God's will. Though he calls them here 'God's elect', he does not exclude others from salvation. One of the chief points in this treatise is that the sinful should not despair but pray for the miracle of regeneration. **42.** *her own.* The world's own.

AN INQUISITION UPON FAME AND HONOUR

1-6. Some abstract thinkers, ignoring the lessons of experience, fabricate a false image of human virtue and on the strength of this they despise fame. Such an idea discourages men from undertaking deeds which might bring advantage to the state and at the same time it does nothing to improve their moral nature. **13-18.** The reason for which these philosophers dismiss fame, that it is a vain thing, applies equally to all human activity. Nevertheless they claim that human nature can attain by its own resources to true virtue. They aspire to an impossible ideal of human behaviour, as though each man were his own god, whereas, in fact, he is full of sin. **24.** Samson (*Judges* 16) destroyed God's enemies by using God-given strength. These men destroy only themselves. **25-30.** The attitudes described are themselves vain-glorious and they lead to attacks on others. All human activities share these characteristics and one kind of skill or learning commonly seeks to enhance itself by disparaging others. **33-6.** Ill destroys good and builds nothing in its place. Its operation is simply destructive and it makes no contribution to useful exchange of ideas. The doctrine of man's self-sufficiency is a vanity created out of nothing and hence without substance, but its promoters try to substantiate it by attacking other people. **60.** *man's worth.* What man calls worth, fame.

A TREATY OF WARS

14. *Irus.* A beggar of Ithaca in *Odyssey* XVIII who became proverbial for his poverty. *Croesus.* The last king of Lydia, renowned for his power and wealth. **15.** Dionysius the younger, tyrant of Syracuse until he was ousted, spent his last years in Corinth, keeping a school. **16.** Agathocles, a potter of Syracuse, became king of Sicily.

ALAHAM

The source is the *Itinerary* of Ludovico di Varthema, first published in 1510, but Greville makes major modifications in the story. His handling of some of the scenes is extremely effective. Peter Ure in a very valuable article on Greville's dramatic characters (*Review of English Studies*, 1950-1, pp. 308-23) described Hala's last speech (the second extract here) as 'a terrible passage, so powerfully written that it almost justifies French Senecanism'.

Chorus Secundus

At this point in the play, Alaham has set in motion his plot to gain the crown and Hala, his wife, has begun to scheme to destroy Alaham and put her lover, Cain, on the throne. Both plots meet a temporary set-back when Cain and his fellow-pasha, Mahomet, stand out against the evil suggestions which have been made to them by Alaham and Hala. The chorus of Furies discusses this, to them, unsatisfactory situation and what they say provides the moral background to this story of murder and passion. Greville's excellent end-stopped couplets sometimes anticipate Dryden in their use of antithesis and balance for climax and anti-climax.

39-40. The reference is to the lines on astronomical maps, showing the courses of heavenly bodies. **47.** While I propose large general plans of action, you spend your time on small details. **73.** I am the foundation on which you all build and so I am also your head. **82.** The fall of man occurred when he ceased to obey the dictates of Right Reason. Ever since, his reason has been corrupt and has engendered all sorts of vice. **85-94.** Corrupt Reason has enough perception to see that man is not wholly a prey to evil, though whether this is because of some extra-human restraining power or because man is not strong enough to carry his wicked tendencies to their logical conclusion, he is unable to decide. The Furies have power enough to cause havoc in Ormus (the setting of *Alaham*) and they can afford to wait for results since lateness is a concept without meaning to immortal beings. **99-102.** Corrupt Reason gives a fair appearance to all the Furies by presenting them as the products of reason. Corrupt Reason is expressed through malice, craft, etc. and they are really all one indivisible body. **105-6.** Roman augurs were religious officials who interpreted omens and advised on the conduct of public business according to their findings. Greville's point is that they have no real access to religious truth and only their staff of office distinguishes them from other men. In *Caelica* XCIII Greville says that the augurs themselves did not believe in their powers. **112.** Men can get away with anything now: the only disqualification for success is fear. **123.** Circe is a beguiling witch in *Odyssey* X. When men drank from her magic cup they were changed into swine. **142.** The third chorus of *Mustapha* contrasts Time and Eternity. We are probably meant to remember here that 'Time shall have a stop'.

Act V, sc. iii, ll. 128-46

These lines spoken by Hala, Alaham's wife, are the last lines of the play. They bring to a close the intense scene in which Alaham, dying of the poison with which his gown is impregnated, pleads desperately with Hala to spare the life of his child. At his death she laments that his torment could not be protracted longer. When she finds that she has killed the wrong child, she is at first altogether confused and loses the sense of fierce purpose which drives her on; but she dismisses self-pity and summons fresh fury to sustain her. In the last lines she assumes a demonic majesty as she invokes the spirits of hell and goes proudly and defiantly to death.

128. This is addressed to the dead child whom she loved because Cain was his father. The empire is the kingdom of death in which they will 'live'. **129.** *This work.* The dead body of Alaham. **132–5.** *The state.* Ground, territory. Hala thinks of the Furies as being born from woman's womb. As she kills herself she invites them to re-enter. There is an implied reference to the story of Adam and Eve. The devil first tempted Eve and she afterwards betrayed Adam. In the play, Hala has deceived Alaham and corrupted Cain. **140.** Hala, and Cain's child, will leave the world of living men whose passions are inadequate and will join the unrestrained furies of hell. **145–6.** She kills the second child and will exchange his ghost in hell for that of Cain's son whom she sent to his death with Alaham.

MUSTAPHA

Among the sources Greville may have used for this play is a version of the story by Hugh Goughe based on the first known European account by Nicholas Moffan, a Burgundian. Goughe's volume, *The Offspring of the House of Ottomano*, was printed in London (1570?) and includes, as well as Moffan's story of the death of Mustapha, an account of the 'customs, rites, ceremonies, and religion of the Turks', translated from Bartholomaeus Georgievitz, a Hungarian who had lived in Turkish captivity for 13 years. Greville may also have learnt a great deal about Turkey from the *Relazioni Universali* of Giovanni Botero. This was published in parts in 1591–6 and translated into English by Robert Johnson as *The Travellers Breviat* in 1601. William Painter also translated Moffan in the hundredth story of his *Palace of Pleasure* (1566) and extracts from his account are printed in Appendix 2. For a further discussion of Greville's possible sources see *Poems and Dramas of Fulke Greville* ed. G. Bullough, ii, 9–25. S. C. Chew's book, *The Crescent and the Rose* (1967), contains a good deal of information about the historical and literary aspects of the relations between Islam and England during the Renaissance.

The manuscripts and early editions show that composition was in two major phases. The unauthorised edition of 1609 (Q) and the manuscripts at Trinity College Cambridge (C) and at the Folger Library represent an earlier and shorter version of the play. The Warwick manuscript (W) and the edition of 1633 (F) represent a later version in which the order of scenes and the treatment of much of the material is altered. This later version gives a completer and more successful account of the implications of the story as Greville saw them, and it is the version which is printed here.

Act I, scene i

20. *kindness.* Kinship. **30.** *in courses popular.* Currying favour with the people. **32.** *art, or kind.* Deliberate policy, or natural to him. **36.** Conduct about which any ruler will be sensitive. **46–8.** Yet supposing it were true that all the world is desirous to obey us, in monarchies which are rather over-large than too small, the king should be judge of how much can be brought together under his sway. **62–3.** Fear of losing you makes me wish for death but fear of leaving you makes me wish for life. **66.** The early versions and W have an interesting alternative reading: 'That reins of all the world's desire bears.' **84–6.** Rossa grants that there may be only few of those opportunists who snatch the advantage of the moment without thinking of the future; but she reminds Soliman of man's propensity to discontent and his love of novelty. **87–8.** Who would choose to be in the place of a man whose life depends on the self-restraint of the wicked? **92.** Men hope for the fulfilment of their wishes through princes' children. **95–8.** Rossa urges Soliman that in a corrupt world self-interest is the best policy. He replies that it is truer wisdom to put God foremost in one's mind. **106.** *Slight.* Sleight. **113.** *kindness.* Natural characteristic. **115.** *providence.* Foresight, anticipation. **125.** *hardly.* Closely.

Scene ii

14. Rossa's unspoken words. **37.** *mystery.* Secret policy. **43.** *ruth.* Mischief, ruin. **57.** Procrustes, a robber killed by Theseus, either stretched the limbs of his victims or cut them off, in order to make them fit the bed to which he tied them. **74–5.** *humorists.* Those who are unreliable or irresponsible e.g. Rosten. People of inferior rank ('below') are blinded by hope and fear and so unable to judge the activities of such as he. **78.** It is Rosten, the 'crafty slave', who is 'careless'. **84–6.** These lines are spoken aside. Rossa is concerned only with satisfying her own will and does not care at all about right or wrong. **95.** *Pluto's kingdom.* Hell. **120.** He scorns what he pretends to worship and grudges the obedience he pays. **125.** *undertakers.* Supporters. **144.** He acts for the public good. **161.** *Basha.* Pasha. **172.** *the port.* The Court. **191.** *mufti.* Priests. **209–19.** Soliman distinguishes between his son and the inferiors who surround him and who are ready to support him in insurrection if he gives the lead. **222.** *oppresseth spirits.* Represses the bold and active.

In the earlier version of this scene Soliman describes a vision seen by the chief priest which depicted life as 'A chaos both of reason, sense and passions' and he comments that his own uncertainties about Mustapha confirm the truth of this:

> Truth methinks speaks both with him and against him,
> And as for reason that should rule these passions
> I find her so effeminate a power
> As she bids kill to save, bids save and doubt not,
> Keeping my love and fear in equal balance.
> That I with reason may think reason is
> A glass to show not help what is amiss. (C text)

The act ends with the Chorus Sacerdotum (end of Act V in the revised text) which picks up the idea that man is torn between passion and reason.

Chorus Primus

The bashas, or pashas, were counsellors, the caddies, or cadis, were judges. These officers of Soliman's state analyse their own position and that of others like them. Seduced by the apparent glory of high office, they flatter tyrants and help them to crush the people's liberties. At the same time, they sell their own self-respect and honour. Greville heaps image upon image to give force to his condemnation of government under a corrupt monarch and he achieves some striking effects. The fact that the speakers are operators of the system they despise and hate gives an added edge to what they say. Towards the end, as they proceed in their analysis and contrast the real position with an imagined ideal of a good king served by uncorrupted ministers, the possibility of revolution is hinted at (175–82) though there is no suggestion that it will lead to a better order.

1. *humours*. The cardinal humours are the four chief fluids of the body (blood, phlegm, choler and melancholy). There were thought to be corresponding humours (forms of moisture or damp exhalation) in the constitution of the external world and these produced meteorological conditions. **35.** We maintain or found colonies at the expense of the native land. **37.** *idle visions*. Promises of future wealth and greatness. **63.** *Lesbian*. cf. Aristotle, *Ethics* v. x. 7: 'For what is itself indefinite can only be measured by an indefinite standard, like the leaden rule used by Lesbian builders; just as the rule is not rigid but can be bent to the shape of the stone, so a special ordinance is made to fit the circumstances of the case'. Greville's point is that the rules are changed according to the sultan's whim. **77.** *confound*. Confuse and ruin the people and ourselves. **85.** Unlike Adam, because Adam in Eden gave the animals their proper names. *Genesis* 2, 19–20. **88.** People are the treasury on which a king draws for his supplies. **90.** The king can rightly make nobles and award new offices. (James I made a lucrative business out of creating baronetcies for those who paid his price.) **92–4.** Virtuous men can be *too* virtuous and forget that the king is the measure of all things. **99–101.** The Court of Chancery had, as Greville says, no power to settle questions of title to land but it could compel defendants to attend its sessions—if necessary, by imprisoning them until adequate sureties were given for their continued presence in court. (W. J. Jones, *The Elizabethan Court of Chancery*, 1967.) **125.** *prerogative*. Sovereign right, subject to no restriction or interference. James I tried to assert this. **144.** *complexions*. Physical constitutions. **163.** *woe worth*. Woe betide. **183–210.** An extended image drawing a great deal of power from its evocation of the treachery of the sea.

Act II, sc. i

14. Who thinks the acme of pleasure is to be robed in purple, the symbol of power and rank. **15.** *castle*. This is the reading of all the earlier texts but W and F have Castile, which would suggest a governor of one of the provinces of the kingdom of Castile. **20.** *the four forgotten monarchs*. Constantinople had fallen to the Turks, the Mameluke rulers of Egypt had been defeated, Greece and Hungary had been overrun. **27.** Achmat is Soliman's chief minister. **53.** *his life is ruth*. His life will be full of remorse. **55.** *fancy-law*. Whims.

Scene ii

1. *popular.* Of the people. **12–13.** Under Soliman I the Turkish empire reached the zenith of its power and prestige. Belgrade, Rhodes and Budapest fell to Turkish arms and Soliman twice besieged Vienna. At his death the empire extended from the frontiers of Germany to the frontiers of Persia, and North Africa was also under Turkish sway. **44.** Diseased limbs are amputated. **50.** *Advantageous ambition.* Ambition nurtured by an advantageous position, like Mustapha's. **51.** *still.* Always. **94.** *nature's laws.* e.g. that sons love their fathers, **96.** Occur at very long intervals. **107.** Step-mothers are proverbially 'wicked'. **121.** It is safer to trust the majority. **137.** Achmat is referring to the advantage which Rossa takes of Soliman's love for her. **150.** *even he.* Zanger, Rossa's son. **165.** To be innocent is not the same as to be foolish. Innocence may include the wisdom of the serpent. **167.** *crudities.* Undigested thoughts.

Scene iii

3. They are insatiably thirsty, like those swollen with dropsy. **17–22.** Camena's divided loyalties are expressed here. Her desire to protect Mustapha conflicts with her loyalty to her mother and her husband, and she knows that to save Mustapha is to deprive Zanger, also her brother, of his chance of succession. **55.** *serene* (serein). A fine rain falling after sunset and thought of as a noxious dew or mist. **57.** The Beglerby is the messenger. **80.** The C, Q, and Folger texts clarify the meaning, adding 'To make it greater and the better known'. **83.** Soliman is not agreeing with Camena but he is advancing a contrary opinion of his own. **98.** Doubt of the heir's loyalty may disturb rightful succession. **104–5.** Things which we desire and which may easily occur often seem out of the question; why should our fears make us believe impossible things are easy? **107–9.** Monsters do not occur without some extraordinary preparation; they are the product of a combination of malign circumstances. **118.** *kind.* Natural bonds. *precipitate.* Ready to rush down to destruction. **159–60.** Where fear is master and where time leads only to death. The son cannot endure to wait for passage of time to give him his inheritance. His impatience makes even his hope a misery, his unsettled state of mind having deprived him of all legitimate sources of happiness. **161.** *custom.* Habit of evil. **170–99.** In this discussion of justice and mercy as arms of government, Greville is handling the same theme as Shakespeare in *Measure for Measure*, especially in Act II, sc. ii, the first interview between Angelo and Isabella. The early version has an interesting extension of Camena's speech. Instead of ll. 182–3 it reads (there are some unimportant variants in the various texts):

> Martyrs few men can be even for the good;
> As few dare seal their mischief with their blood.
> The prince's wisdom and his office this,
> To see from whom, how far each one can move,
> To find what each man's God and devil is,
> Judging and handling frailty with love.
> For ignorance begetteth cruelty,
> Misthinking each man everything can be.
> The best may fall, the worst that is may mend.
> You hedge in time, and do prescribe to God,

> Where safety, not amendment you intend.
> The last of all corrections is the rod,
> And kings that circle in themselves with death
> Poison the air wherein they draw their breath.

173. Which finds the folly that lies deep in all men. **186–7.** Theseus cursed his son, Hippolitus, and Neptune carried out the curse. The reference is apt, since Hippolitus was the innocent victim of a stepmother's malice. **210.** Not true, of course, but Camena respects her mother. **226–7.** If Soliman takes a wrong step now he exposes himself to danger from his son and his life will be at risk, as Mustapha's is.

Chorus Secundus

This chorus of priests ranges very widely. It treats of the relations between church and throne, the contrast between states dedicated to an active role (this means primarily war) and those who cultivate learning and contemplation, the decay of greatness, and a comparison between the open tyranny of the Turkish régime and the covert ways by which in Christian countries laws are bent to serve power. The chorus is dramatic in that it presents the Moslem point of view and contrasts Christian and Moslem practices to the advantage of the latter. Greville seems to have been influenced, here and elsewhere, by a work on the Ottoman empire published in Paris in 1588 by René de Lucinge. It was translated by Sir John Finett in 1606 as *The Beginning, Continuance and Decay of Estates*. In the chorus, the priests consider the particular situation of Soliman and Mustapha and conclude that Mustapha's submission to his father is an example of the way in which people allow kings to abuse and degrade them. The chorus is full of thought and there are telling lines but it reads as though it may be a patch-work made up of parts of earlier poems. The fact that at l. 121 the stanzaic form gives place to couplets reinforces this impression. The C and Q texts have no chorus at the end of Act II but the Folger ms. has a short chorus which urges man to 'examine what life is' and to welcome death.

19–22. Ali was fourth in order of the caliphs or successors of Mahomet. The question of his right to succeed divided the Mahomedan world into two great sects, the Turks denying it and reviling his memory. The priests here claim that they 'lovingly' adjudicated in the dispute. **52.** *sovereignty.* Sovereignty. Here, as elsewhere in the play, the extra syllable is required in the line. **70.** *To keep . . . self-humour.* To gratify some vanity. **74.** *courts.* Courts of law. **79.** *cell-bred sciences.* Theoretic learning. **85.** *dreaming nation.* Christians overrun by the Turks. **107–8.** Selim I, Soliman's father, had rebelled against his father and was almost certainly responsible for his murder. He also had his two elder brothers executed. **116.** Rulers keeping control of institutions ostensibly designed to restrain them. **124.** *den.* Defensive position. **131–8.** The Turks exercise summary justice: Christians adopt lengthy legal processes which are nevertheless not impartial since they must defer to the interests of the monarch. **153–4.** Tudor history illustrates these changes. **165–6.** The Turks did not try to convert conquered peoples but taxed them if they did not conform. **168.** If it were not for their lack of power, which they miscall modesty. **175–6.** They are no more important than the particles of dust seen in a sunbeam, or some small disturbance in the life of an individual which has no effect on the world at large (the phrasing of 176 is ironic).

Act III, sc. i

56–9. We shall gain nothing by direct attack on Soliman's love for his son. We have to play on his instinct for self-preservation and make that the stronger emotion. **113.** Honour is only a matter of convention and what is acceptable depends on the humour of the tyrant. **114.** *speak doubtful.* Speak ambiguously. **120.** *His lightness.* (Presumably) his honesty.

Scene ii

10–14. cf. Hala's speech in *Alaham*, Act v, sc. iii (p. 64). **38.** *Avernus.* A lake, thought of as the mouth of hell.

Chorus Tertius

There is a great sweep and energy of thought in this chorus which is a striking piece of philosophical verse. Greville takes a familiar theme but in contrasting time and eternity he is not concerned with the beauty or the pathos of mutability. He concentrates entirely on the vanity of earthly perspectives when seen *sub specie aeternitatis.* Eternity is willing to see Mustapha sacrificed to the pressures of time because his eternal destiny will not be affected by such events. They are significant only on the worldly scale. The C text has no chorus for this act but Q and the Folger ms. have the Chorus Tartarorum, which the revised version puts at the end of Act V. In the earlier version it immediately follows the scene between Mustapha and Heli which in C, Q and the Folger ms. is Act III, sc. 5. There are some important variants in the earlier text of this Chorus which are noted in the commentary to the Chorus Quintus, Tartarorum.

20. *probabilities.* Guesses at truth. **31–2.** Agathocles of Sicily, once a potter. **57.** *stamps.* Coinage is guaranteed by the ruler's symbol stamped on it. **61–6.** People of power in the state have undertaken to bring about the death of father or son. They keep their purpose hidden and try to promote false advice. But their selfish machinations are confused by their necessary dependence on chance and occasion. **65.** *occasion.* Opportunity which time controls. **67–70.** Shall I, because this misdeed comes to pass in time and because future evil will follow from present ill (so that disorder does not prosper) be held responsible for man's will to do wrong? **76.** *centre of defect.* Nothing. **82–4.** The image of Time reflected in her mirror shows progressive deterioration. **85.** Emblematic representations of Eternity sometimes show it as a serpent with its tail in its mouth. Such images imply that eternity has no end. In giving this form to Time, Greville wishes to denote that it is self-enclosed, bound to a sequence of events which it cannot escape. **93.** Mortals mistake the true nature of eternity as mariners and others may miscalculate the true position of the stars. **97.** A minute is the limit of her existence. **100.** The present moment is the link between these two. **128.** *brick-wall.* Cause to rebound. **136.** Cadmus sowed the teeth of a dead dragon and from them armed men grew, who fought and killed each other till only five were left.

Act IV, sc. i

1. At the end of Act II, sc. iii, Soliman was going with Achmat to the church to seek guidance in his uncertainty about Mustapha. Act IV, sc. i may be supposed to take place in the mosque. Achmat is dismissed, and Soliman, who has sacrificed (27) now sees visions. **6.** Are they products of his own mind or messages from heaven? cf. Macbeth whose troubled conscience also produced visions: 'Is this a dagger which I see before me?' (II, i). **8–20.** Soliman sees a vision of an angel bearing a mirror in which the unflattering truth about himself and his actions is revealed. The vision itself seems to be preceded by a warning inscription (8–12). **28.** He has lost confidence in what he is by seeing what he should be.

Scene iii

70. e.g. A figure in the 'tens' column is worth ten times more than if in the 'units' column. **85.** *guidon.* A flag or pennant, broad at the end next the staff and forked or pointed at the other end. Camena has embroidered a picture upon this showing Saturn eating his children (lest they destroy him) and by word and image warning Mustapha of his danger and urging him to take measures to avert it. **95.** *waste.* Uncultivated, natural. **103.** *characts.* Letters. **115.** As if she felt only his harms. **124.** Phaeton, off-spring of the sun-god, drove his father's chariot across the sky one day. He was too weak to control the horses and Zeus killed him with a flash of lightning. **127.** *spirits of practice.* Intriguers.

Scene iv

1–31. These lines do not occur in the earlier version of the play. In the revised version they serve to underline the essential choice with which the characters are faced, between the service of God which is true religion, on the one hand, and politic subservience to power on the other. The quasi-theological language which the Beglerby uses (idol, grace, merit, image, saint, martyrs) makes Greville's point that man's instinct to worship and serve is perverted by sin into an instrument of corruption and selfish cynicism. The extension of the Beglerby's part in this scene also brings him into relation and comparison with Heli, the priest, during the climactic interview with Mustapha. The Beglerby represents secular authority which chooses power before virtue. Heli represents institutional religion which, contaminated by its connection with the state, has also chosen the false god of power. Heli has a tenderer conscience than the Beglerby, for he regrets his part in Mustapha's doom, but he has no stronger sense of a true, other-worldly religion. In Q and the Folger ms. the 'Chorus Tartarorum' follows immediately after this scene (Act III, sc. v in the earlier texts) and in this position it sums up very aptly the naturalistic arguments which Heli opposes to the religious attitudes of the unworldly Mustapha. **67.** C and Q and the Folger ms. have 'But rooted ill brings no remorse with it' which clarifies the meaning. **77–8.** Rather than forgive after the event, prevent the event taking place. To let it occur, with its dire consequences, is to make 'mercy' more severe than law. **106–8.** The C, Q and Folger texts are clearer:

> Where guilty people shall live in good name,
> The guiltless only live and die with shame.

116. *cockatrice.* Basilisk, a fabulous serpent. **173.** Mustapha addresses his retinue. **208.** *Divan.* The Turkish privy council. **223.** *popularity.* Popular or democratic feeling.

Chorus Quartus

This chorus is a commentary on the decline of empire which, characteristically, traces the stages of decay from the fall of angels and of men, and through the creation of 'the outward church' by which truth is perverted and men are enslaved. In time, monarch and church, from being mutual supports, become rivals. Law fails to settle their disputes and war ensues. Crown, church, law and army being all then at odds with one another, the bonds of society are loosened and the way is open for the people, cynical now about their masters, to take matters into their own hands. In the Q text in place of this chorus, there is another, spoken it seems by Death, urging men not to be afraid of dying. C has a more extended version of this chorus which includes the lines which appear in the Folger ms. as the chorus to Act III. These are also about death. At the end of Act IV the Folger ms. has the first fourteen lines of the C chorus which have not appeared before. (The C Chorus is printed in Appendix 1.) The material of Act IV in the earlier version is different. The scene between Mustapha and the priest takes place at the end of Act III and Act IV is concerned with reports of Mustapha's death and some immediately following events.

32. Icarus was the son of Daedalus. Daedalus made wings, which were attached to the body with wax, and he and his son set out to fly from Crete to Italy. But Icarus grew ambitious and flew too near the sun so that the wax melted and he fell into the sea. **75.** *Mars his seed.* Soldiers, whose duty is to kill one another. **85.** *four complexions.* The four cardinal humours of the body. **87.** *fold.* Fail, or falter. **93.** *Mavors.* Mars.

Act V, sc. ii

2. *raised equality.* Kings and tyrants are no more than other men by nature but merely elevated to a higher place. **22.** *to wage.* To engage or employ. **23.** *sect.* Sex. **24.** *misconster.* Misconstrue. **33.** *power.* Troops, armed followers. **84–8.** Mustapha's speech is given special emphasis in W by being written in a large italic hand not used elsewhere in the play.

Scene iii

9. Having lost faith in monarchy, they take authority to themselves. **15.** Cf. *Amos* 4, 11: 'Ye were as a brand plucked out of the burning'. **16.** *Acheron.* A river of the underworld, round which the shades of the dead hover.

Scene iv

30. *sect.* Faction. **48.** What arguments can be effective on one who voluntarily chooses to be swayed by passion?

Chorus Quintus, Tartarorum

See note to Act IV, sc. iv, **1–31.** There is a copy of the 1633 folio of Greville's works in the Bibliothèque Nationale with manuscript annotations in the margin against this chorus and the Chorus Sacerdotum. The hand has been identified as that of Sir Kenelm Digby and it is probable that he helped Greville's executor, Sir John Coke, with the editing of the poems. See W. Hilton Kelliher, 'The Warwick Manuscripts of Fulke Greville' in *The British Museum Quarterly*, xxxiv, 107–21.

1. Q and the Folger ms. read 'Religion, thou vain and glorious style of weakness'. The Bib. Nat. copy has this ms. note: 'In the original it is, Blind Religion, thou glorious et cet. But this seemed too atheistical to be licensed at the press'. **10.** Q and the Folger ms. read ' Mankind! trust not this dream, religion'. In the Bib. Nat. copy, 'superstitious' is underlined and 'religious' is written in the margin. **14–15.** Q and the Folger ms. read:

> No, no thou child of miracles begotten,
> Miracles that are but ignorance of causes.

The alterations of the earlier text may have been made out of fear that the original would be too strong for publication. **24.** *table*. Writing tablet.

Chorus Sacerdotum

In C and Q and the Folger ms. this chorus occurs at the end of Act I where it serves to comment on the 'self-division' which Soliman is experiencing. It does not occur in the W text, and in F it is separated from the rest by a deep ornament. It is doubtful whether Greville himself intended it to remain. The ms. marginalia in the Bib. Nat. copy make this comment: 'This chorus is misplaced; but rather than lose it, I caused it to be inserted here to fill up this page'. As it is, the opening lines are perhaps the best known part of Greville's work and the two choruses together, of Tartars and of Priests, make a comparison which is central to the play. The Tartars express a view of life which is entirely bounded by this world and they are cynical about all religious claims. The priests profess more, but do not really feel it in their hearts. In effect, they accept the worldliness of the Tartars. 'Nature' is not for them the simple rule of self-preservation and self-indulgence it is for the Tartars but their perspectives are nevertheless mortal and the faith which would take them beyond self-division and transform their experience of life is ultimately beyond them. The same comparison between the avowedly secular and the professional religious is made in Act IV, sc. iv when the attitudes of the Beglerby and Heli are laid bare. As in that scene so in these choruses, a contrast is made explicitly or implicitly between these men and the saintly Mustapha whose life and death are illuminated by an inner light and who really believes in the other-worldly values of the religion he professes.

There is no chorus at the end of the play in the C and Q texts. The Folger ms. repeats the chorus on death which it has already used at the end of Act II.

21. 'God and stir' is the reading of C and the Folger ms. Q and F read 'good and still'. It is difficult to decide between these. 'God and stir' makes obviously good sense but 'good and still' could be defended as a description of unquestioning devotion.

LIFE OF SIR PHILIP SIDNEY

The *Life* was first published in 1652 and its first editor gave it the present title. Oblique criticism in the text of aspects of James I's policies and conduct point to a date of composition between 1604 and 1614 when Greville was out of office, and a reference to the death of Henry IV of France, which took place in 1610, seems to give a more precise indication of the time of writing. It is likely, however, that the original matter, dedicating his poems to the memory of Sidney, was an early stratum and that other layers of material were added to the composition at a later date or dates.

I. The purpose of this 1585 expedition to the West Indies was to damage Spain by striking at the source of her wealth. Greville tells brilliantly the story of Sidney's participation and ultimate frustration and brings sharply into focus the principal characters: Sidney, eager for high and heroic exploits, Drake, calculating and devious, and himself, a cool and shrewd observer, watching over his friend's interests.

11-12. Sidney's position as an officer in the Ordnance Department, and also his circle of friends and connections, enabled him to be of great service in preparing the expedition. **15.** *dispense with.* Allow. **51-2.** *dare I not . . . misprision of time.* I dare not say that his mismanagement of time was due to ulterior motives. **54.** *mean-season.* Meantime. Don Antonio was a pretender to the Portuguese crown. He received some support from Elizabeth. **58.** *his father-in-law.* Sir Francis Walsingham. **64.** Achates was the faithful friend of Aeneas—*fidus Achates* in the *Aeneid.* **83.** *to discover . . . being discovered.* To make our presence known without our being aware of his betrayal. **87.** Mercury was Jove's herald. **93.** *yet did he . . . process.* He ignored this first formal command. **98.** *his uncle.* The Earl of Leicester. The 'grace' Sidney was offered was the governorship of Flushing. **102.** *selfnesses.* This is Nowell Smith's emendation which makes good sense and would be characteristic of Greville; but the texts which Smith collated and the Shrewsbury ms. read: 'self places'.

II. This extract is the source of the famous story of Sir Philip Sidney's gesture of compassion to the poor soldier wounded in the same battle as himself. His act of courtesy and consideration made a deep impression.

12-13. The English action at Zutphen was in fact directed to stopping provisions entering the town. **16.** *his.* His armour. **17.** *the marshal of the camp.* Sir William Pelham. **18.** *Themistocles.* According to Plutarch, the triumph of Miltiades at Marathon so stirred Themistocles' envy that he could not sleep. **20.** *cuisses.* Armour protecting the front part of the thigh. **23-5.** The English had expected only a small force of Spaniards and they themselves numbered some 500 men. When the mist cleared they found themselves confronting 3000 or more. Later other troops came out of the town to protect the convoy and the English withdrew. **28.** *rampiers.* Ramparts. **31.** *misprision.* Mistake. **36.** Sidney received his wound at the second charge of the English horse. **49.** Sidney was taken from the camp by river to Arnheim that same afternoon.

III. Greville here brings together his main claims for Sidney. It is characteristic of his political interests that he does not omit to point out the political use fulness of such a man to his prince. In the paragraph which immediately follows this extract he contrasts the 'true worth' of Sidney with the more usual qualities of men of rank and eminence who are preoccupied only with self-glorification and have no noble personal qualities to match their station. The passage, like many others in the *Life*, implies a contrast between Sidney and the men on whom James I lavished his favours.

6. *Zephyrus*. The west wind. **7.** Maecenas was the patron of Virgil and Horace. His name has come to stand for generous and enlightened patronage. **16.** *engineer*. Inventor. **25.** *humorous*. Awkwardly disposed, or eccentric. **33.** *unequal nature and education*. Both by innate qualities and the training he had received, Sidney was superior to the rest. **37-8.** *that contemptible army of dwarfs*. The pigmies who attacked Hercules when he lay sleeping after his defeat of the giant Antaeus.

IV. Greville's account of the downfall of Essex follows on from his explanation of why he destroyed a play he had written about Antony and Cleopatra (see extract VII). He writes warmly of the malice and trickery by which he believes Essex was destroyed and he makes a vigorous defence of his career and his essential probity. The remarks about favourites at the end return to a familiar theme in the *Life*.

3. *sect-animals*. Members of a political faction. **6.** *passive postures*. Attitudes resulting from pain or irritation. **7.** *sovereign's circles*. The royal prerogatives. **20.** *his kinsman*. Greville and Essex were distantly related. **21.** *remora*. The sucking-fish which the ancients believed could arrest the movement of any ship to which it attached itself. **23.** *figurative*. Imaginary. **24.** *prosopopeias of invisible rancour*. Figments created by the disguised malice of Essex's enemies. **29.** Jupiter was the lord of heaven. Pluto was the god of the underworld, or Hades. **34-5.** *unreturning steps*. The reference is to the fox's reply to the lion in Horace *Epistles* I, i: 'The footprints frighten me, because they all face towards your den and none away from it.' **40.** The admiral Greville has in mind is probably Sir Walter Raleigh, a prominent member of the faction led by Robert Cecil. Cecil was 'a creator of admirals' and it is he whom Greville holds primarily responsible for Essex's downfall. **53.** *competency*. Rivalry. **57.** *Henry III*. King of France. **62-3.** *predicaments*. Situations. **69.** *the envious . . . party*. The Shrewsbury ms. reads: 'selfness, envy or faction'. **77.** *Integrities*. Uncorrupted state.

V. This passage is part of a lengthy digression concerning the reign of Queen Elizabeth. Greville writes of her domestic and foreign policies and of the principles by which, he claims, she governed. He praises her as a model of wisdom and skill in government—'that wonder of Queens and women'. His admiration was no doubt genuine but the terms of his praise often suggest, as in this extract, simultaneous criticism of James for misjudgement and mismanagement.

2-3. *under-earth buildings*. Deeply founded institutions, especially the estates of the realm. **5-6.** *time-authorised assemblies*. Parliament. **11-15.** The Queen's long experience of government, which is far more valuable in dealing with the affairs of men than book-learning, enabled her to foresee likely consequences. **16-18.** Greville has put the point a different way a little earlier: 'Neither did she, by any curious search after evidence to enlarge her prerogatives royal, teach her subjects in Parliament by the like self-affections, to make as curious inquisition among their records to colour any encroaching upon the sacred circles of monarchy . . .' **21.** *forcing humours.* The habit of exercising compulsion. **29.** Remus jumped over the newly-built wall of Rome: Elizabeth's England was a newly-built Anti-Rome because she had established the Protestant church after the Roman Catholic rule of her sister. **31.** *genius.* Natural capacity. **40.** *after-game.* A second game played to better the result of the first; hence a change of plan when something goes wrong. **61.** *captiving.* Captivating.

VI. Greville refers to his attempts to see service abroad and the quashing of these by Elizabeth. These attempts culminated in his taking service under Henry of Navarre in 1587 and this, as he explains in the *Life*, earned him six months banishment from court. The passage from which the extract is taken thus establishes the period and the circumstances in which Greville began to write poetry and it identifies Sidney as the dominating influence. Though Greville does not mention his short poems in the *Life*, some of the *Caelica* sequence belonged to the earliest period of composition.

   9. *that excellent governess.* Queen Elizabeth. **26–7.** *this kind of writing.* Poetry.

VII. Greville's comments on his own works, brought together here, are of great interest though they do not, unfortunately, clear up uncertainties about dates of composition. The date of the *Life* is itself uncertain and Greville's remarks here may refer to versions of the treatises and plays earlier than those we have now. These comments provide good examples of Greville's prose style, highly individual like his poetry and, at its best, charged with a kind of dark splendour.

   19–20. Greville changed their places by removing them from the plays. **24.** *essays.* First attempts, rough drafts: but Greville may have had in mind his friend Francis Bacon's use of the word. In the dedication of his essays to Prince Henry, Bacon describes them as 'certain brief notes, set down rather significantly than curiously', i.e. with more care for substance than stylistic adornment. **28.** Nothing is known of Greville's play about Antony and Cleopatra apart from this reference. **33.** *the astronomer's pit.* Plato in *Theaetetus* tells how Thales, the astronomer, fell into a well as he was looking at the stars. This story became a Renaissance commonplace. **38–48.** Ovid's *Metamorphoses* told stories of men and women transformed into animals and vegetables. Greville interprets these as indicating that hostile circumstances may impose upon men a false image which belies their true natures. He saw this kind of distortion and misrepresentation take place when Essex, who had been worthy of the love hitherto bestowed on him, was condemned as a traitor and executed. Greville thought it best not to allow possible imprudencies in his play to expose him to similar hazard. **64.** *ill talent.* Hostile inclination. **70–1.** Sophocles and Euripides seem to be the wrong way round, either by scribal error or Greville's own. **74.** *casual.* The plots depend on chance or accident. **83–5.** *my noble friend.* Sidney. Greville thought of Sidney's translations of religious works by Du Plessis Mornay and Du Bartas, and his translation of the Psalms, as his 'real' works and *Arcadia*, his prose romance, as merely a marginal production. **89–92.** Sidney was in process of revising his first version of *Arcadia* when he went to the Low Countries in 1585. He left a ms. of the revised version, as far as it had gone, in Greville's care, and Greville supervised the printing of the incomplete text in 1590. **97.** *On whose foot the black ox had not already trod.* Greville is adapting a proverbial expression for experience of care or sorrow.

APPENDIX 1

Below is the chorus on death which appears in full as the chorus to Act IV of *Mustapha* in the C text and parts of which are included in the Q edition and the Folger ms. With its emphasis on attitudes to death, the chorus picks up a central motif of the play. The text is that of C:

When will this life's spark put in our spirit
To give light to the lamp of flesh and blood
Leave to deny strong destiny her right
Which it feels daily cannot be withstood.
Man, look not down. Look up into the sky.
There live you must, and may be glad to die.
Be not bewitched, as thoughts in error be:
I am no tyrant. I am nature's child.
Life needs not fear that honest comes to me.
My terrors are to life that is defiled.   10
Yet if blind ignorance herself could see,
The wicked that hard hearts against me build
May know that since I come not by election,
As I end joys, I end all imperfection.
Man dream no more: examine what life is.
It is a stage whereon desires show
By passions' war, flesh is no seat of bliss.
It is the way wherein desires go
From present time, where she is still amiss,
To times past and to come for ease of woe,   20
Only well pleased when it is well forgotten,
With long repentance and short joys begotten.
Since death therefore is all already past,
The heaven where old age must find his rest,
Since life in living hitherwards makes haste,
Since nature there renews equality,
Since power and fortune under her are placed:
Let beasts repine, and men be glad to die;
For mean estates must stand in fear of many
And great are cursed for that they fear not any.   30

1–6. These are the lines which Q prints as the chorus to Act IV. **1–14.** These are the lines which the Folger ms. has as the chorus to Act IV. **15–30.** These are the lines which the Folger ms. has as the chorus to Act II and also at the end of the play. **23–4.** Since everything which is in the past is already dead, and since death is the heaven where old age will find rest. **25.** The second word is missing in C but the Folger manuscript supplies 'life'.

Mufti. Which answer of repulse so excited the inflamed affections of the king as, setting all other business apart, he caused the Mufti to be sent for. And, giving him liberty to answer, he demanded whether his bondwoman being once manumised, could not be known carnally without violation of the laws? Whereunto Mufti answered, that in no wise it was lawful, unless before he should with her contract matrimony. The difficulty of which law in such sort augmented the king's desires as, being beyond measure blinded with concupiscence, at length agreed to the marriage of the said manumised woman and after the nuptial writings according to the custom were ratified and that he had given unto her a dowry, 5,000 Sultan ducats, the marriage was concluded, not without the great admiration of all men, especially for that it was done contrary to the use of the Ottoman lineage . . . This manumised woman, being advanced through fortune's benefit, was esteemed for the chief lady of Asia not without great happiness succeeding in all her affairs. And for the satisfying of her ambitious intents there wanted but only a mean and occasion that after the death of Soliman one of her own children might obtain the empire. Whereunto the generosity and good behaviour of Mustapha was a great hindrance—who indeed was a young man of great magnanimity and of wit most excellent, whose stomach was no less courageous than he was manly in person and force. For which qualities he was marvellously beloved of the soldiers and men of war, and for his wisdom and justice very acceptable to the people. All which things this subtle woman considering, she privily used the counsel of Rustanus for the better accomplishing of her purpose, knowing that he would rather seek the advancement of his kinsman and the brother of his own wife, as reason was, than the preferment of Mustapha with whom she certainly knew that Rustanus was in displeasure.

[Rossa and Rustanus begin their plots to poison Soliman's mind against his son but the good behaviour and high repute of Mustapha give them nothing to work on. Rossa then sends poisoned garments to Mustapha but Mustapha makes one of his slaves don the garments first and so escapes the trap. At last news is received that Mustapha is considering marriage with the king of Persia's daughter. Rossa and Rustanus see their opening here and persuade Soliman that this marriage alliance with an ancient enemy of the Ottoman line is part a scheme to join the might of Persia to that of Mustapha's own troops and their aid kill and supplant Soliman. Soliman is convinced and sends Rustanus into Syria under pretext of a Persian invasion, with orders either to bring Mustapha back as a prisoner or to kill him by any means he can. Rustanus fails the attempt but Soliman becomes even more determined to kill Mustapha.] year following he commanded an huge army to be levied, once again proclamation that the Persians with a greater power would invade therefore thought it meet that he himself, for the common safeguard, ought personally to repair thither with a power to withstand the of his enemies. The army being assembled, and all the furnitures that behalf, they marched forwards and, within a few days after, the followed. Who being come into Syria, addressed a messenger to command him forthwith to repair unto him, then being encamped yet Soliman could not keep secret the mortal hatred he bore to ers, although he employed diligent care for that purpose, but

APPENDIX 2

From *The Palace of Pleasure* by William Painter (1566).

Be it known therefore, that Soliman had of a certain bond woman this Mustapha, to whom from his youth he gave in charge the country of Amasia. Who with his mother continually resident in the said country, became so forward in feats of arms as it was supposed of all men that he was given unto their country by some heavenly providence. This Mustapha, with his mother being placed in the said country, it chanced that the king his father was beyond measure wrapt with the beauty of another of his concubines called Rossa, of whom he begat four sons and one daughter . . . The fourth [son was called] Jangir, whose surname, by reason he was crook-backed, notwithstanding his pregnant wit, was Gibbus. And the daughter he bestowed in marriage upon Rustanus Basha, who . . . exercised the office of Vesiri . . . (which office we use to call the president of the council) and according to his natural disposition of covetousness, abusing the said office, altered and changed all manner of thin belonging to the same . . . In the meantime this Rossa, of whom mention is n before, perceiving herself before others to be beloved of the king, under the of religion declared unto the Mufti (which is the chief bishop of Ma religion) that she was affected with a godly zeal to build a temple an for strangers, to the chief God, and honour of Mahomet, but she was to attempt the same without his advice. And therefore she asked same would be acceptable to God and profitable for the hea Whereunto Mufti answered that the work to God was accept her soul it was nothing available. Adding further, that not on was at the king's disposition, but her life also, being a bon fore that work would be more profitable to the king. V woman in her mind daily being troubled, became ve was void of all comfort. The king being advertised began to comfort her. affirming that shortly he w should enjoy the effect of her desire; and forthw her free, a writing and instrument made in custom, to the intent she might not be at con in bondage. Having in this sort obtained thi mass of money determined to proceed i season, the king, without measure bei Rossa, as is aforesaid, sent for her b court. But the crafty woman, unsl with subtle answer, which was th to call to his remembrance as w own laws, and to remember s not deny but her life remai carnal copulation to be ha without committing of s the same to be feigned o.

that the knowledge thereof came to the ears of one of the Bashas and others of honour. Amongst whom Achmat Basha privily sent word to Mustapha to the intent he might take the better heed to himself. And it seemed not without wonder to Mustapha that his father without necessary cause should arrive in those parts with so great a number. Who notwithstanding, knowing himself innocent, although in extreme sorrow and pensiveness of mind, determined to obey his father's commandment although he should stand in danger of his life. For he esteemed it a more honest and laudable part to incur the peril of death in obedience to his father than live in contumely by disobedience. Therefore in that great anxiety and care of mind, debating many things with himself, at length he demanded of a learned man which continually was conversant with him in his house . . . whether the empire of the whole world or a virtuous life ought rather to be wished for. To whom this learned man most godly answered: That he which diligently weighed the government of this world shall perceive no other felicity therein than a vain and foolish appearance of goodness. 'For there is nothing', quoth he, 'more frail or unsure than the world's prosperity. And it bringeth none other fruits but fear, sorrow, troubles, suspicions, murders, wickedness, unrighteousness, spoil, poverty, captivity, and such like which to a man that affecteth a blessed life are in no wise to be wished for. For whose sake whoso list to enjoy them loseth the happiness of that life. But to whom it is given from above to weigh and consider the frailty and shortness of this state (which the common people deemeth to be a life) and to resist the vanities of the world at length to embrace virtue, to them truly in heaven there is a place assigned and prepared of the highest God, where he shall inherit perpetual joys and the felicity of the life to come.' With which answer Mustapha, being somewhat pricked in conscience, wonderfully was satisfied as being told of him which seemed by a certain prophecy to prognosticate his end. And tarrying upon no longer disputation, immediately directed his journey towards his cruel father . . . And at his arrival to the camp, so soon as he had pitched his tent, he apparelled himself all in white and putting certain letters in his bosom which the Turks use to do when they go to any place . . . he proceeded towards his father, intending with reverence (as the manner is) to kiss his hand. But when he was come to the entry of the tent, he remembered himself of his dagger which he wore about him and therefore ungirding himself he put it off for avoiding of all suspicion. Which done, when he was entered the tent, he was very courteously (with such reverence as behoved) welcomed of his father's eunuchs. And when he saw no man else but the seat royal, where his father was wont to sit, ready furnished, with a sorrowful heart stood still and at length demanded where his father was. Who answered that forthwith he would come in presence. In the mean season he saw seven dumb men (which the Turk useth as instruments to keep his secrets and privily to do such murders as he commandeth) and therewith immediately was wonderfully mased saying: 'Behold my present death'. And therewith stepped aside to avoid them; but it was in vain for, being apprehended of the eunuchs and the guard, was by force drawn to the place appointed for him to lose his life and suddenly the dumb men fastened a bowstring about his neck. But Mustapha, somewhat striving, required to speak but two words to his father. Which when the wicked parricide his father heard, beholding the cruel spectacle on the other side of the tent, rebuked the dumb men, saying:

'Will you never execute my commandment and do as I bid you? Will you not kill the traitor which these ten years space would not suffer me to sleep one quiet night?' Who, when they heard him speak those cruel words, the eunuchs and dumb men threw him prostrate upon the ground and cording the string with a double knot, most pitifully strangled him'. [Soliman then sends for Jangir, the crookback]: who was ignorant of that was done, and, jesting with him as though he had done a thing worthy of commendation, bade him go and meet his brother Mustapha; who with a joyful cheer made haste to meet him. But when he came to the place and saw his unfortunate brother lie strangled and dead upon the earth, it is impossible to tell with what sorrow he was affected. And he was scarce come to the place but his wicked father sent messengers after him to tell him that the king had given him all Mustapha his treasures, horsemen, bondmen, pavilions, apparell: yea, and moreover the province of Amasia. But Giangir, conceiving extreme sorrow for the cruel murder of his dear brother, with lamentable tears spoke these words: 'Oh cruel and wicked dog, yea, and if I may so call my father, Oh traitor most pestilent, do thou enjoy Mustapha his treasures, his horses, furnitures and the said country too. Is thy heart so unnatural, cruel and wicked to kill a young man so notable as Mustapha was, so good a warrior and so worthy a gentleman as the Ottoman house never had or shall have the like, without any respect of humanity or zeal natural? By saint Mary, I need to take heed least hereafter in like manner thou as impudently do triumph of my death being but a crookback and a deformed man'. When he had spoken these words, plucking out his dagger, he slew himself.

[Various tumults in the state follow these events. Achmat Basha calms the soldiers in the first instance but eventually Soliman has to face them in person. Rossa and Rustanus withdraw in fear of their lives to Constantinople and Soliman repents of his deed. Painter ends by recalling the prowess of Mustapha and adds, making a striking change of view from that which has been apparent so far: 'Therefore we have good cause to rejoice for the death of this cruel enemy that should have reigned and to think the slaughter of him not to be done without God's special providence who in this sort hath provided for us.']